Six Spices
A Simple Concept of Indian Cooking

SIX SPICES

A SIMPLE Concept of INDIAN Cooking

NEETA SALUJA

JONES
BOOKS
Madison, Wisconsin

Jones Books
309 N. Hillside Terrace
Madison, Wisconsin 53705-3328
U.S.A.
www.jonesbooks.com

First edition, first printing

Library of Congress Cataloging-in-Publication Data

Saluja, Neeta.
  Six spices : a simple concept of Indian cooking / Neeta Saluja.
     p. cm.
  Includes bibliographical references and index.
  ISBN-13: 978-0-9763539-9-7 (alk. paper)
  1. Cookery, Indic. 2. Cookery (Spices) I. Title.
  TX724.5.I4S265 2007
  641.5954—dc22

                                       2007012275

Printed in China

To my mother, Maheshwari Mathur,
who gave me my first lessons in Indian cooking
and remained a guiding and nurturing force during my formative years.

CONTENTS

1. All about Spices

2. Seasoning with Hot Oil *(Tel ka Chounk)*

Using hot oil as a cooking medium for seasoning. • Blending spices in certain sequences to release their full flavors. • Adding seasoned oil to flavor salads, rice, and *raita*. • Cooking vegetables in seasoned oil to add flavor.

Recipes

3. Seasoning with Hot Ghee *(Ghee ka Chounk)* .31
Using hot ghee to flavor beans and lentils. • Preparing seasoning with herbs and spices using ghee as a cooking medium. • Simmering beans and lentils with seasoning to achieve their full tastes.

Recipes

4. Cooking with Powdered Spices *(Sookha Masala)* 57
Different techniques for cooking vegetables with powdered spices. • Using spices in a certain order and at a specific time to achieve unique tastes.

Recipes

5. Cooking with Curry Paste *(Peesa Masala)* 87

Preparing curry paste (*masala*) with fresh ingredients and spices. • Roasting curry paste to perfection. • Simmering meat and vegetables in *masala* to make perfect curries.

6. Beyond the Basics: Recipes to Complete the Meals 115

Understanding Indian cuisine. • Recipes to round out an Indian meal. • Recipes using spices other than the basic six.

7. Tips and Techniques 153

Use of appropriate kitchen equipment and cooking utensils. • The characteristics of ingredients such as curry leaves, coconut, and lentils. • Instructions for preparing uncommon ingredients such as *paneer*, ghee, and bean sprouts.

ACKNOWLEDGMENTS

I want to thank the many people who encouraged and supported me throughout the process of visualizing and writing this book. My husband, Kewal, my daughter, Sonali, and my son, Saurabh, inspired and cheered me on as I created and wrote down the recipes. They were always enthusiastic and willing partners as we tried new ones. I'm especially grateful to Saurabh and Sonali, who helped by reading the chapters as I wrote them. And thanks to all my friends and students who relished my cooking and willingly offered their feedback.

Thanks to Joan Strasbaugh, my publisher, who had faith in my idea and trusted me. Thanks to Elizabeth Kramer, who guided me through the editing process, and to Karen Johnson Mathews, who helped with the tedious task of reading the recipes to ensure accuracy in their presentation. Both of them offered support and were very gracious in their reading and editing of the manuscript. Thank you to Kashmira Sheth for her encouragement during the formative steps of this book. Thanks also to Laura Kearney, the book's copy editor, for making the process of editing fun and simple for me.

For the photo shoot, I would like to thank the following: Whole Foods Market, for providing the food; Orange Tree Imports and All Through the House, for the props; Suchi Kantamneni, for offering her place; Alka Arora, Nithya Hariharan, Lisa Mattingly, Kalpana Patel, Divya Sharma, and Sudha Sirohi, for their help and support. And special thanks to Martha Busse, the photographer, David Bacco, the food stylist, and Janet Trembley, the book designer.

INTRODUCTION

When I arrived in Australia from the city of Bhopal in the central province of India, the weather was cold and blustery. I felt alone in an unfamiliar land and among people I did not know. I thought I knew English, but in Sydney it was spoken with an accent that was hard for me to understand. Almost immediately, I regretted leaving friends and my native land. But these feelings soon passed as I was reunited with my parents, who had immigrated to Australia the previous year. Once I arrived, I was happy to learn that my mother had kept the Indian traditions alive. To welcome me, she had prepared a hearty meal of hot simmering dal, steaming rice, spicy curry, and warm chapatis. What a wonderful surprise!

To make this meal, Mom had special ordered the spices, lentils, and other essential ingredients from India. Every few months she would have them shipped so she could continue to serve us food that was familiar. She quickly learned to adapt her recipes by incorporating local ingredients and fresh produce into her daily cooking. We began to enjoy vegetables like broccoli, brussels sprouts, and zucchini prepared with the spices we'd always known.

That was back in the 1970s. In recent years, ethnic food has become tremendously popular. Besides Italian, Chinese, and Mexican restaurants, we now see Thai, Turkish, Japanese, and Indian cuisine available in towns and cities across the United States. Today, both casual diners and connoisseurs can enjoy the spicy and aromatic Indian cuisine. Some Indian restaurants serve authentic dishes while others offer fusion foods, adapting and combining ingredients and techniques from different cultures and countries to make even more creative menu offerings. In my travels, I've tasted a hint of curry powder in many pasta dishes served at Italian restaurants in Japan. Japanese supermarkets sold a special curry mix to prepare a popular Japanese curry-rice dish. And the renowned Restaurant Raji in Memphis creates French-Indian fusion delicacies.

In the last few years, I have noticed a surge in the number of Indian restaurants in my adopted home of Madison, Wisconsin, and in neighboring towns. New specialty stores and even grocery chains are offering good selections of spices, beans, basmati rice, and other essential food items from India. Accessibility and availability of these ingredients used in Indian cooking have instilled a desire in Americans to venture into a new world of cooking with spices. They long to learn to create the mouth-watering curries they've tasted at Indian restaurants and to incorporate more beans and lentils into their diets. Coriander and cumin become part of their collection of spices. Some simply want to learn new culinary skills.

Driven by the increased interest, food stores, cooking schools, and community colleges are offering cooking classes in ethnic cuisine and bookstores are carrying a wide selection of ethnic cookbooks. When I began searching for a good Indian cookbook, however, I found that most were written either as memoirs with few recipes or as books with scores of recipes. Those recipes often consisted of long lists of spices and unfamiliar ingredients combined with little instruction on how to use them. The various regional cuisines of India created further confusion for a beginner. Finding the right Indian cookbook was both challenging and overwhelming.

Encouraged by the keen interest of my many friends and students in my cooking classes, I decided to write a reliable Indian cookbook with simple, easy-to-follow instructions for some of my favorite authentic recipes. Although basic enough for beginners, my recipes will still inspire the creativity of more seasoned cooks.

Keeping clarity and simplicity in mind, I developed a unique way to present my recipes, relying on basic spices and similar cooking techniques. In my own kitchen I often use fewer spices than called for in a recipe, so the recipes I selected require no more than six spices to create tasty dishes. Most of the recipes are based upon four cooking techniques: seasoning with hot oil, seasoning with hot ghee, cooking with powdered spices, and cooking with curry paste.

In chapters 2 through 5, I give you an overview of each technique. The recipes that follow have been tested and tasted many times throughout my fifteen years of teaching experience. After twenty-five years of sampling my recipes, my family and friends still look forward to my meals.

I have included an additional chapter of recipes, "Beyond the Basics," with my favorite breads, snacks, drinks, and desserts to complete a meal. The "Tips and Techniques" chapter contains detailed information about uncommon ingredients and instructs you on how to use them.

My hope is that this book will become a valuable resource as you experience the joy of Indian cooking. With it as your guide, you soon will be preparing simple and satisfying home-cooked, Indian-style meals. Each recipe is sufficient to feed four people. To serve more, you can easily double the amounts.

Six Spices: A Simple Concept of Indian Cooking introduces you to the concept of spices and guides you in the preparation of healthy, delicious authentic Indian meals.

Shubharambh (pleasant start)!

CHAPTER 1
ALL about SPICES
The role of spices in traditional Indian culture

A steaming cup of ginger tea on a cold, foggy

winter morning is a great incentive to jump out of bed and leave the comfort of a warm quilt. Ginger tea gives us the needed warmth to keep a cold or cough away. During hot summer months, cumin or cardamom added to a yogurt drink helps keep our bodies cool. We use *ubtan*—a paste made with turmeric, oil, and flour—on our faces and bodies before we take a bath. Turmeric gives an exceptional glow to our skin and its antibacterial properties keep our faces clear of blemishes.

In India, we grew up with spices as an integral part of our lives. No written formulas or notes were kept for us to follow. It is the experiences of our elders and their eagerness to lovingly and carefully share their knowledge that has kept this art alive over many centuries. As we observed our mothers and grandmothers, we learned the traditions of our culture.

Buying, using, and storing spices

In many Indian households, spices are bought in bulk at the market after the harvest, when they are cheaper. They are dried, pounded, and stored at home so they are readily available throughout the year. Today they are also conveniently available prepackaged at many specialty stores.

Most spices have a long shelf life when stored properly. Here are some tips to keep spices fresh for a long time:
- Store in dry, airtight, glass containers.
- Keep in dry, dark, and cool places.
- Handle with dry hands and dry spoons. Moisture can spoil the spices.

Descriptions of the most common spices

The six essential spices I used in developing my recipes are listed below. I discuss each spice in detail to help you understand its origin, quality, and usage in Indian cooking.

Asafetida (*hing*). A spice with a pungent and peculiar smell. It is collected as a sap from the stem and roots of plants from the Umbelliferae family. When dried, asafetida crystallizes and becomes hard. In crystal form, it is yellowish brown and has a stronger smell than in its powdered form. When powdered asafetida is mixed with ingredients such as rice flour, the spice becomes more mellow and is less potent.

Powdered asafetida is available prepackaged. It produces a strong aroma when added to hot oil or ghee. The smell is comparable to garlic and is often used in cooking as a substitute for onion and garlic, especially as a flavoring spice by people in India who are following a diet that excludes these. Asafetida is frequently used with beans, lentils, and certain vegetables to aid digestion and reduce flatulence. As a home remedy, it is often rubbed on the stomach of a colicky baby to reduce discomfort.

Chilies (*mirch*). A variety of dried and fresh fruits of plants of the genus *Capsicum* and the Solanaceae family, also called peppers. The young fruit is green; as it matures, the color changes to red. Many varieties of chili peppers are available around the world, ranging in color and intensity of flavor. When added to food, chilies give a sharp, fiery taste. They help to stimulate the digestive system and promote increased blood circulation and metabolism. The antibacterial properties of chilies help preserve food for longer periods of time.

Green chilies vary in their degree of potency. You'll learn through trial and error which is right for you. The taste varies from the mild, sweet Japanese Shishito pepper, to the medium-hot Hungarian pepper, to the very hot cayenne pepper and the extremely fiery habanera pepper. The shape and size also varies from the thin and small Thai peppers, to the long and slender cayenne pepper, to the long and plump banana pepper. Some peppers are round, like the small cherry pepper and the large and plump bell pepper. Peppers are pale yellow or light green when young. When mature, peppers are bright yellow, orange, red, dark green, or purple depending on the variety.

Chilies can be used fresh, dried, crushed, or powdered. You can find them in the produce and spice sections of grocery, Indian, and many other ethnic food stores. Most dishes from the Indian subcontinent use chili powder in their preparation.

Fresh green chilies are often ingredients in salads and seasonings. When buying chilies, choose those with shiny and smooth skins; these are the freshest. Green chilies refrigerate well for eight to ten days. To store, remove the stalks, wrap in paper towels, and place in an air-tight container.

Dried whole or crushed chilies are often added to hot oil or ghee, imparting a pungent and sharp smell and infusing the oil or ghee with a roasted, smoky flavor. The seasoned oil or ghee is then used to spice up lentils, salads, and vegetable dishes.

Chili powder is prepared by pounding the dry whole chilies and then finely grinding them. The powders vary in degree of potency, from mild to medium to very hot. Chilies from the Kashmir region are very mild and are often used with stronger chili powder to make curries. When added to curries, this chili powder imparts a red pigment during the slow cooking, giving a peculiar red color to the curry. Southern states and the states of Gujarat and Rajasthan supply the hotter varieties of chili powder.

Take special care when handling chilies. The pith and the seeds are the hottest parts. Many people use gloves while working with chilies. After handling chilies, be sure to wash your hands well with soap. Avoid touching your nose, mouth, and eyes for a few hours. It is the oil from the chili that causes the burning sensation.

If affected by chili burns, wash your skin thoroughly with cold water and soap. Gently dry the area with a soft cloth and apply unsalted butter, ghee, vegetable oil, or skin cream. It may take anywhere from a few minutes to a few hours to completely diffuse the burning sensation.

To reduce the intense heat in the mouth after eating a chili, remove all food and chew a piece of bread or eat plain rice. Follow with a drink of cold milk—which will also reduce any burning in the digestive tract and stomach.

Coriander (*dhania*). An aromatic plant belonging to the Umbelliferae family. The leaves and seeds of the coriander plant are used extensively in Indian cooking. Its fresh leaves and young stems add fragrant flavor to a variety of dishes and make an attractive garnish. Coriander powder is an important spice in curries and curry powders. In traditional medicine, coriander is often used for its antibacterial and flatulence-relieving properties.

Coriander seeds are harvested at the end of the growing season and are dried in the sun before use. The seeds are yellowish brown and spherical in shape, slightly smaller than whole black peppercorns. They release a roasted, earthy smell when cooked in hot oil or dry roasted.

Coriander powder is a basic and frequently used spice. Seeds must be completely dried before grinding into powder. The powder is light brown with a mild and sweet taste. Coriander powder adds savory flavor to curries and helps thicken the gravy. Both coriander seeds and powder are available in the spice sections of grocery and many ethnic food stores.

Fresh coriander (*hara dhania*). The fragrant leaves and shoots of the coriander plant; known as cilantro in the United States. The cuisine of countries such as India, Mexico, and Thailand use cilantro. When added during cooking, the aromatic chopped fresh leaves and stalks add color and freshness to any dish. When finely chopped, they are a beautiful garnish. Cilantro is an essential ingredient in many salads and chutneys.

Cilantro is available year-round in produce sections of grocery and many specialty food stores. It is often sold in bunches with roots, stems, and leaves. To store cilantro, remove the roots and thick stems. Spread it on a paper towel to let the moisture evaporate; turn stalks over after ten minutes and repeat. Wrap cilantro in the paper towel, place in a plastic container or plastic bag, and refrigerate. Cilantro will stay fresh up to ten days. Wash cilantro just before using it. Fresh cilantro is always recommended since it looses its effectiveness and aroma when dried or frozen.

Cumin seeds (*jeera*). The aromatic and flavorful seeds of the cumin plant, which, like parsley, is a member the Umbelliferae family. Cumin seeds are one of the essential spices used in seasoning lentils and vegetables. No spice rack is complete without them. The light brown cumin seeds are small and cylindrical with pointed ends and ridges on the skin. Raw seeds are bitter, but roasted or fried cumin seeds have desirable taste and a strong, pleasant aroma.

Cumin seeds can be used raw, fried, and dry roasted. Most lentils are seasoned by frying cumin seeds in ghee. Dry roasted and powdered seeds are used in many yogurt dishes. Powdered raw cumin is used in curries and curry powders.

The mature seeds are harvested and dried in the sun before they are sold at the market. Most grocery and specialty stores carry cumin seeds and cumin powder. Roasted cumin powder is prepared at home and is not available in the stores. (See Chapter 7, page 161.) It is also used in Mexican and some African cuisines.Cumin has a cooling effect on our bodies. It also is used as an aid in digestion.

Mustard seeds (*raai*). The tiny, spherical-shaped seeds from the mustard plant, which belongs to the Cruciferae family and the genus *Brassica*—the same group as common cabbage. Mustard seeds range in color from dark reddish brown to black. Raw seeds have no odor, but the crushed and powdered seeds have a pungent smell and a very sharp taste. Powdered mustard seeds are used in Indian pickles to give a sour taste and help preserve them. Mustard seeds are used to season a variety of lentils and vegetables. To prepare the seasoning, the seeds are added to hot oil or ghee. When heated, they change color from brown black to grayish brown and give a rich, roasted, nutty flavor to a dish.

Oil made from mustard seeds adds authentic flavor to many regional dishes in India. In northeastern India, the oil is used for its pungent smell. Oil from mustard seeds is also used for stimulating body massages and as a hair tonic. Black mustard seeds are not available at regular grocery stores but can be found in Indian stores. In general, yellow mustard seeds are not used in Indian cooking.

Turmeric (*haldi*). A tuberous rhizome used in powdered form for its preservative and medicinal characteristics. This yellow, bitter-tasting spice is a must in Indian cooking. Although it does not add any particular taste to a dish, its antibacterial and preserving properties make turmeric the most important spice in Indian cuisine. It has an acrid smell and gives a peculiar yellow color to the curries.

The underground stem portion of the plant comes from the same family as the popular herb ginger. The roots are boiled and dried in the sun before they are pounded to prepare the turmeric powder. Fresh turmeric is faintly aromatic and is slightly bitter in taste. In many Indian grocery stores, you will find fresh young turmeric for making pickles. This spice is a safe and natural coloring agent for many food preparations. Powdered turmeric is added to curries and commercial curry powder. It is available in most supermarkets.

In *Ayurvedic* medicine, an ancient art of healing in India, turmeric is used for its antibacterial, anti-inflammatory, and healing properties. In modern medicine, scientists are experimenting with turmeric in treatments for cancer, liver diseases, and bacterial infections. In my home, we use it for facial treatments, for making poultices for wounds, and for soothing sore throats. Its use dates back thousands of years, to the Vedic time in India. Turmeric roots also have significant use in religious ceremonies.

CHAPTER 2
SEASONING with HOT OIL
Tel ka Chounk

Chounk is a common word used in Indian cooking
to describe the word "seasoning." Also called *tadka, vaghar,* and *fodni, chounk* gives a
unique taste, flavor, and aroma to food. Seasoning with *chounk* is one of the basic
techniques used by Indian cooks to enhance beans and legumes, which are commonly
known as dal. Many dry vegetable dishes and rice *pullav* (pilaf) are also seasoned with
chounk. Chounk adds zest to bland salads and *raitas* (a mixture of yogurt and raw or
cooked vegetables).

To prepare *chounk,* you may use cooking oil or ghee as the medium for cooking. The
method of preparation is the same for both, but the dishes created are quite distinct in
taste and flavor, so I have created two separate chapters: "Seasoning with Hot Oil" and
"Seasoning with Hot Ghee." In this chapter, I use oil.

Different regions of India use a variety of oils for cooking depending on the cultivated
crop and the taste acquired by the local people. Coconut oil is used in southern India,
peanut oil in the central region, and mustard oil in eastern India. I prefer canola oil
because it is odorless and colorless. Canola oil is also low in saturated fat, which makes
it a healthier choice. However, you can use any oil of your choice.

Chounk is prepared with a combination of certain whole spices, ground spices, and
some fresh ingredients. The spices are added to hot oil in a certain sequence, giving each
spice a chance to fully release its flavor in a timely fashion without burning or being
undercooked. Also, you want to be sure that the oil is sufficiently hot to ensure the
complete release of flavors; without sufficient heat, the spices will be hard, undercooked,
and bitter. Fresh ingredients are added after the whole spices, and ground spices are
added last.

This method of seasoning is used in two different ways. In the first, *chounk* is
prepared first and then vegetables are added and cooked in the seasoned oil. In this
process the vegetables absorb the full flavor of the spices while cooking, becoming
deliciously rich in taste. The spices impart not only great flavor to the vegetables but also
help preserve them for longer periods of time.

In the second method, *chounk* is prepared in the usual way and added to the dish at the end. For example, the *chounk* is poured over and mixed with a prepared salad, *raita*, or rice. Using *chounk* is a simple way to season foods and give them a tasty final touch. With a little variation, the spices and the sequence in which they are added give a unique taste and aroma to each dish.

In an Indian household, everyday cooking can easily be done with six basic spices. Sometimes however, you may want to use additional spices to complement a particular vegetable, to make other regional dishes, or to create a special family recipe. The limited use of the six spices in this book should not keep you from experimenting with other spices. These spices are the building blocks for creating your own collection of spices.

Preparing *chounk* with hot oil

When preparing *chounk*, use a small covered frying pan or a saucepan. For cooking vegetables, select a covered, nonstick pan. The size of the pan will depend on the amount of vegetables.

In most cases, I add whole spices to the hot oil first, followed by the fresh ingredients and finally the powdered spices. Whole spices are added first because they need the hottest temperature to release their flavors. After adding the whole spices, reduce the heat to medium. Add the fresh ingredients, such as onion, ginger, garlic, and chopped chilies. Cook lightly until fresh ingredients become soft. Powdered spices, such as chili powder and asafetida, are added last to avoid burning or scorching them and to retain their flavors. This sequence is important. If not followed, the spices will either be undercooked or burned.

Before heating the oil, you should have all the ingredients ready in the order in which the recipe calls for them. Place pan on the stove with the required amount of oil at medium-high heat. Heat the oil to a high temperature. To check the temperature of the oil,

OBSERVATIONS and Helpful Tips

- The measured amount of spices is only a guideline. Alter the amount according to individual taste.

- When using onion and garlic in a recipe, you generally will not use asafetida in the seasoning.

- Cover the pan while cooking to retain the best flavor and aroma and to reduce cooking time.

- Take care when handling chilies. Removing seeds from the chilies reduces their potency.

The following spices and fresh ingredients are used in this chapter for preparing *chounk*.

SPICES	FRESH INGREDIENTS
Asafetida	Curry leaves
Cumin seeds	Green chilies
Dry red chilies	Garlic
Mustard seeds	Ginger
Red chili powder	Lemon
Turmeric	Onion
	Tomato

drop a few mustard seeds or cumin seeds into the hot oil. The seeds should sizzle and come to the oil's surface right away. If they don't, wait a few more seconds and repeat.

As a rule, add the mustard seeds first to the hot oil. It's important to cover the pan immediately after adding the seeds to prevent splattering. (Mustard seeds tend to pop and jump when heated.) Keep covered until the seeds stop popping, then add other whole spices such as cumin seeds or whole dry chilies. Reduce heat to medium, and add fresh ingredients. Cover the pan until splattering stops. If onions, ginger, or garlic are used, cook until onions become soft or until garlic and ginger are lightly browned. Remove the pan from the heat. Add the desired ground spices to the oil according to the recipe. Let the spices sizzle in the hot oil so they can release their flavors. The prepared *chounk* can be poured over and mixed with cooked rice, *raita*, or salad. Or raw vegetables can be added to the prepared *chounk* and then cooked with the seasoned oil.

I want to emphasize again how important it is to a recipe's success that you carefully follow the order in which the ingredients are to be used and the method for preparing each recipe.

SIX SPICES: A Simple Concept of Indian Cooking

RECIPES

Spinach and Red Potatoes
Palak Lal-Aalu ki Subji

New red potatoes and fresh spinach make an excellent combination. Frozen spinach can be substituted for fresh. A simple variation is to add onion or garlic to the seasoning to give a new flavor to the dish.

INGREDIENTS
1 pound red potatoes, washed
4 tablespoons cooking oil
$1/2$ teaspoon cumin seeds
3 broken dry red chilies
$1/4$ teaspoon red chili powder
$1/4$ teaspoon asafetida
2 16-ounce packets of frozen or fresh spinach
1 teaspoon salt or to taste

METHOD
1. Peel and cut potatoes into $1/2$-inch cubes.
2. Heat oil in a heavy, medium-size frying pan. When oil is hot, add cumin seeds and reduce heat to medium. Add dry red chili pieces, chili powder, and asafetida. Cook for another 30 seconds.
3. Add spinach and let cook on medium-high heat until most of the water has evaporated. Add potatoes and salt. Stir and cover the pan. Reduce heat to medium and cook until potatoes are cooked.
4. Serve with hot chapati or steamed rice.

Green Beans with Coconut
Hari-Faliyan Nariyal ke sath

This dish, with fresh, tender beans mildly flavored with hot oil seasoning, is one of my favorites to cook. Coconut adds a sweet nutty taste to this dish. The availability of fresh coconut year-round in southern India makes this dish one of the more popular ones in that part of the country.

INGREDIENTS
2 pounds fresh green beans
3 tablespoons cooking oil
1/2 teaspoon mustard seeds
3 broken dry red chilies
1/4 teaspoon asafetida
1 teaspoon salt or to taste
1/4 cup fresh shredded coconut (See Chapter 7, page 160)

METHOD
1. Wash and string beans. Cut them finely into 1/4-inch pieces.
2. Heat oil in medium-size frying pan over medium-high heat.
3. When oil is hot, add mustard seeds and cover the pan. Reduce heat and wait until seeds stop popping.
4. Add dry red chili pieces and asafetida and cook for another 30 seconds.
5. Add cut beans and salt. Stir them well to coat the beans evenly with the seasoning.
6. Reduce heat to medium and cover the pan. Cook beans, stirring occasionally to avoid sticking and burning, until they are tender and soft.
7. Stir the shredded coconut into the beans and remove pan from the heat.
8. Serve hot or cold as an accompaniment to the meal.

SIX SPICES: A Simple Concept of Indian Cooking

Green Mustard and Radishes

Hari Sarson, Muli ke sath

This dish has a unique combination of vegetables. In winter, it's popular in northern India, where these vegetables are in abundance. Fresh spinach can be substituted for mustard greens.

INGREDIENTS

2 bunches (2 pounds) mustard greens
2 medium-size white radishes (can substitute with red salad radishes)
3 tablespoons cooking oil
1/2 teaspoon cumin seeds
3 broken dry red chilies
1/4 teaspoon red chili powder
1/4 teaspoon asafetida
1 teaspoon salt or to taste

METHOD

1. Wash and chop the mustard leaves.
2. Peel and cut radishes lengthwise into quarters. Cut each piece into 1/2-inch slices.
3. Heat oil in large frying pan over medium-high heat. When oil is hot, add cumin seeds and reduce heat to medium. Stir in dry red chili pieces, red chili powder, and asafetida. Cook for another 30 seconds.
4. Add radishes and stir them into hot oil seasoning. Gradually add chopped mustard leaves into the pan. Cover the pan and cook for 10 minutes or until mustard leaves are wilted.
5. Add salt and mix it well into mustard leaves and radishes. Cover the pan and reduce heat to medium. Cook until most of the juices are evaporated and radishes are well cooked.
6. Remove the lid and increase the heat to medium-high. Cook the greens further to remove any excess moisture and to give a roasted flavor to the dish.
7. Serve hot or cold as a side dish with rice and lentils.

Curried Dry Potatoes
Sookhe Aalu ki Subji

Potatoes are very versatile and are used in almost every dinner or lunch menu. You can make a potato dish in a short time by seasoning with one or two spices. Some other potato dishes become very elaborate and elegant when cooked with many spices and prepared using several steps, which adds to the amount of time required to make it. This potato dish is a popular version from southern India.

INGREDIENTS
4 large potatoes (about 2 pounds)
3 tablespoons oil
1/2 teaspoon black mustard seeds
1/2 teaspoon urad dal
2 to 3 dry red chilies
1 small onion, chopped
8 to 10 curry leaves
1/2 teaspoon turmeric powder
1 teaspoon salt or to taste
1/2 cup water

METHOD
1. Boil and cool potatoes. Use fork to break them into small chunks.
2. Heat oil in a heavy frying pan. When oil is hot, add mustard seeds and cover the pan immediately. Once the popping stops, reduce heat to medium. Add urad dal and red chilies; fry for a few seconds.
3. Add chopped onions and curry leaves; fry until onions become soft. Add turmeric powder and cook for another 30 seconds.
4. Add potatoes and salt. Stir mixture until potatoes are coated with spices.
5. Gradually stir in water.
6. Cover the pan and reduce heat to medium-high. Cook for 5 to 10 minutes, stirring occasionally.
7. Serve hot or at room temperature as a side dish.

Carrot Salad
Gajar ka Salad

Sweet-and-sour carrot salad is one of my family's favorite salads. It makes a perfect complement to a lentil and rice meal. You can assemble and season this salad in advance. Add salt and sugar just before serving to maintain the crispness.

INGREDIENTS
2 cups carrots, grated
1 green chili, diced
2 teaspoons lemon juice
1/2 teaspoon salt or to taste
1 teaspoon sugar

SEASONING
2 teaspoons cooking oil
1/4 teaspoon black mustard seeds
1 dry red chili
4 to 5 fresh curry leaves

METHOD
1. Place carrots, chili, and lemon juice in a mixing bowl; mix well.
2. Heat oil in a small frying pan. When oil is hot, add mustard seeds. Cover the pan and remove it from the heat.
3. When mustard seeds stop popping, return the pan to the stove. Add red chili and curry leaves. Immediately pour the seasoned oil over carrots and cover.
4. After 1 minute, mix well and store it in an airtight container.
5. Just before serving, add salt and sugar; mix it well. Serve the salad cold.

Cabbage and Tomato Salad
Patta-gobhi, Tamatar ka Salad

This is a quick and simple way to serve a salad for a large crowd. Cabbage with tomato is the perfect choice, but substituting coleslaw mix for the cabbage makes this great tasting salad simpler to put together. Prepare just before serving to retain its freshness.

INGREDIENTS
4 cups shredded cabbage or coleslaw mix
1 large ripe tomato, diced
1 green chili, diced
2 tablespoons lemon juice
3/4 teaspoon salt or to taste
1 teaspoon sugar

SEASONING
2 teaspoons cooking oil
1/4 teaspoon black mustard seeds
1 dry red chili
4 to 5 fresh curry leaves

METHOD
1. Place all ingredients in a mixing bowl except salt and sugar; mix well.
2. Heat oil in a small frying pan. When oil is hot, add mustard seeds. Cover and remove pan from the heat. When the popping stops, return the pan to the stove.
3. Add red chili and curry leaves to hot oil. Immediately pour the seasoned oil over the cabbage and tomato mixture and cover.
4. After 1 minute, mix well and store it in an airtight container.
5. Just before serving, add salt and sugar; mix it well.

Sprouted Mung Bean Salad
Ankur wali Moong Dal ka Salad

This salad has variety of textures, tastes, and flavors. It makes a healthy side for a vegetarian or nonvegetarian menu.

INGREDIENTS
2 cups mung bean sprouts (See Chapter 7, page 159)
1/2 teaspoon salt or to taste
1/4 cup water
1 teaspoon sugar or to taste
1 tablespoon fresh lemon juice or to taste
1 medium cucumber, chopped
1 medium tomato, chopped
1/2 cup red onion, chopped
2 green chilies, chopped
1/2 cup cilantro, chopped

SEASONING
1 tablespoon cooking oil
1/2 teaspoon ginger, grated
1/4 teaspoon red chili powder
1/4 teaspoon asafetida

METHOD
1. Heat oil in a medium-size frying pan on medium heat. Add ginger and stir for few seconds. Stir in chili powder, asafetida, and bean sprouts.
2. Stir for about 1 to 2 minutes. Add salt and water. Cover the pan and reduce heat to low. Cook for 15 minutes or until sprouts are soft.
3. Add sugar and lemon juice. Cook until most of the liquid has evaporated. Cool to room temperature.
4. Mix cooked sprouts, cucumber, tomato, onion, chilies, and cilantro in a bowl. Adjust salt, sugar, and lemon juice according to taste.
5. Serve the salad at room temperature.

Seasoned Mung Beans
Chounki Moong

Crunchy and rich in taste, mung beans are high in protein and carbohydrates. When I was a child, we often were served this as a hot snack with tea. It also goes well with chapati or paratha *(Indian breads).*

INGREDIENTS
1 cup whole mung beans
1 teaspoon salt or to taste
1/4 cup water
2 tablespoons sugar
1 tablespoon fresh lemon juice

SEASONING
2 tablespoons cooking oil
1/2 teaspoon black mustard seeds
1 green chili, chopped (optional)
5 to 6 fresh curry leaves (optional)
1/4 teaspoon red chili powder
1/4 teaspoon asafetida

METHOD
1. Clean and wash beans in cold water. Soak them in warm water overnight.
2. Drain beans and set them aside.
3. Heat oil in a medium-size frying pan on medium-high heat. When oil is hot, add mustard seeds. Cover the pan immediately and wait until the seeds stop popping.
4. Add green chili and curry leaves. Cover the pan quickly. Remove pan from the heat and add red chili powder and asafetida.
5. Add drained beans to the pan and cook them for about 5 minutes, stirring occasionally. Add salt and water. Cook on low heat until beans become soft and tender. More water can be used if needed. Add sugar and lemon juice.
6. Serve the beans hot.

Potato with Mint in Yogurt
Aalu Pudine ka Raita

On hot evenings when you don't want to spend much time near the stove, you should simply serve this potato raita *with boiled rice or rice* pullav. *The fragrant mint and cool yogurt make this a desirable dish in summer.*

INGREDIENTS
2 cups plain yogurt
2 medium-size potatoes, boiled, peeled, and cubed
1/4 cup fresh mint, chopped
3/4 teaspoon salt or to taste
1 teaspoon sugar
1/4 teaspoon red chili powder

SEASONING
1 tablespoon cooking oil
1/2 teaspoon black mustard seeds
2 whole dry red chilies

METHOD
1. Mix yogurt in a bowl to make it smooth.
2. Add potatoes, mint, salt, sugar, and chili powder.
3. Heat oil on medium heat in a small frying pan. When the oil is hot, add mustard seeds. Cover immediately until seeds stop popping.
4. Add red chilies to hot oil and roast them for 30 seconds.
5. Pour hot seasoning over the yogurt mixture; stir well.
6. Keep refrigerated until you are ready to serve.

Tomatoes with Yogurt and Peanuts
Tamatar ka Raita Moongfali ke sath

In mid-summer and at the end of the growing season, when you don't know what to do with so many tomatoes, this recipe comes in handy. The tangy tomatoes, crunchy peanuts, and sour yogurt create an unusual taste and texture. This salad can be served with a western or Indian dinner. Prepare it just before serving.

INGREDIENTS
2 large ripe tomatoes, diced
1 green chili, diced
3/4 teaspoon salt or to taste
1 teaspoon sugar
1/2 cup yogurt
2 tablespoons cilantro, chopped
1/4 cup roasted peanuts, crushed (See Chapter 7, page 165)

SEASONING
2 teaspoons cooking oil
1/4 teaspoon black mustard seeds
1 dry red chili
4 to 5 fresh curry leaves (optional)

METHOD
1. Place tomatoes, chili, salt, sugar, and yogurt in a bowl.
2. Heat oil in a small pan. When the oil is hot, add mustard seeds. Cover the pan quickly and remove from the heat.
3. When the seeds stop popping, return pan to the stove. Add red chili and curry leaves. Immediately pour seasoning over tomato and yogurt mixture and cover.
4. After 1 minute, uncover it. Mix in cilantro and peanuts.
5. Serve at room temperature.

Roasted Eggplant with Yogurt
Bhune Baingan ka Raita

The flavor of roasted eggplant gives an exotic taste to this yogurt side dish. For many gatherings, I have served eggplant raita *as a dip with naan (Indian clay-oven bread) or pita bread, along with fresh vegetables.*

INGREDIENTS
1 cup roasted eggplant pulp (See Chapter 7, page 162)
2 cups plain yogurt
1/4 cup red onion, finely chopped
2 tablespoons fresh cilantro, chopped
1 fresh green chili, chopped (optional)
3/4 teaspoon salt
1 teaspoon sugar

SEASONING
1 tablespoon cooking oil
1/2 teaspoon black mustard seeds
1/4 teaspoon red chili powder

METHOD
1. Mix eggplant pulp with a fork until it is smooth. Add pulp to yogurt.
2. Add onions, cilantro, green chili, salt, and sugar to the mixture; mix well.
3. Heat oil on medium-heat in small frying pan. When oil is hot, add mustard seeds. Cover pan immediately; keep covered until seeds stop popping. Remove pan from the stove.
4. Add red chili powder and pour seasoning over the yogurt mixture and stir.
5. Keep refrigerated until you are ready to serve.

Butternut Squash with Yogurt
Kaddu ka Raita

Butternut squash raita has a unique texture and taste. This is a great side dish for an Indian meal. It also goes well over roasted chicken and lamb, giving the meat an ethnic taste.

INGREDIENTS
1 cup cooked and mashed butternut squash (See Chapter 7, page 160)
2 cups plain yogurt
1 teaspoon salt or to taste
1 1/2 tablespoons sugar

SEASONING
1 tablespoon cooking oil
1/2 teaspoon black mustard seeds
1 green chili, chopped
5 to 6 fresh curry leaves
1/4 teaspoon red chili powder
1/4 teaspoon asafetida

METHOD
1. Mix mashed squash and yogurt in a mixing bowl until mixture is smooth. Add salt and sugar.
2. Heat oil in a small frying pan. When oil is hot, add mustard seeds. Cover pan immediately.
3. After the seeds stop popping, add green chili and curry leaves. Cover pan quickly. Remove pan from the heat and add red chili powder and asafetida.
4. Pour seasoning into the squash and yogurt mixture; mix well.
5. Refrigerate until ready to serve.

Corn and Bell Pepper Rice
Makki, Shimla Mirch ka Chawal

This dish is visually appealing because of the corn and colorful peppers and appetizing thanks to the tangy taste of tomatoes and fried onions. Simple variations using other vegetables make this a versatile recipe.

INGREDIENTS
1 cup basmati rice
2 cups water
1 cup frozen corn
1/2 red bell pepper, diced
1/2 green bell pepper, diced
2 tablespoons tomato paste
1 teaspoon salt or to taste

SEASONING
4 tablespoons cooking oil
1/2 teaspoon cumin seeds
1 cup onions, chopped
1/2 teaspoon red chili powder

METHOD
1. Cook rice in the water. Let it cool to room temperature. Separate rice grains by hand, gently breaking up lumps.
2. Heat oil in a small pan. When oil is hot, add cumin seeds. Stir seeds for a few seconds.
3. Add chopped onions; sauté until onions become soft and translucent. Stir in red chili powder.
4. Add frozen corn; mix corn with the spices and onions. Cover pan and cook for about 5 minutes.
5. Add red and green bell peppers. Cook for another 5 minutes. Stir in tomato paste; mix well.
6. Add rice and salt to the mixture. Cover and cook on low heat for 10 minutes, stirring occasionally until the rice is completely heated.
7. Serve hot with any raita or plain yogurt.

Yogurt Rice
Dahi ka Chawal

Yogurt rice is a simple yet flavorful light meal. The addition of diced cucumber to this recipe makes it a perfect cool summer lunch. Be sure to prepare this a few hours in advance so the seasoning has time to infuse its flavors into the rice.

INGREDIENTS
1 cup long grain rice
1 1/2 cups water
3/4 cup plain yogurt
1/4 cup milk
1 teaspoon salt or to taste

SEASONING
3 tablespoons cooking oil
1/2 teaspoon black mustard seeds
2 dry red chilies, broken
1 green chili, chopped
7 to 8 fresh curry leaves

METHOD
1. Cook rice in the water. Let it cool to room temperature.
2. Mix yogurt and milk until a smooth consistency.
3. Mix yogurt and milk mixture, rice, and salt in a bowl; set aside.
4. Heat oil in a small pan. When oil is hot, add mustard seeds and cover the pan. Reduce heat and wait until seeds stop popping.
5. Add red chili pieces, chopped green chili, and curry leaves. Cover to prevent splattering.
6. Pour seasoning over yogurt and rice mixture. Mix well and cover.
7. Let sit a couple of hours before serving. Serve at room temperature.

Lemon Rice
Neembu ka Chawal

This popular dish from southern India has become one of the rice dishes most favored by my family and friends. The simplicity of preparation and the convenience of serving lemon rice at room temperature make it an excellent item for dinner parties. Important: Be sure to prepare the dish at least two hours before serving.

INGREDIENTS
1 cup basmati rice or long grain rice (See Chapter 7, page 165)
2 cups water
1/4 cup fresh lemon juice
1 teaspoon salt

SEASONING
6 tablespoons cooking oil
1/2 teaspoon black mustard seeds
1/4 cup raw cashew nuts
1 green chili, chopped
1/4 teaspoon turmeric powder
1/4 teaspoon asafetida

METHOD
1. Cook rice in the water. Let it cool to room temperature.
2. Mix lemon juice and salt. Keep aside.
3. Mix 3 tablespoons of the oil into rice grains by rubbing gently to separate rice into single grains.
4. Heat remaining 3 tablespoons of oil in a small pan. When the oil is hot, add mustard seeds and cover the pan. Reduce heat and wait until seeds stop popping. Add cashews and fry until the nuts are light brown.
5. Remove pan from the heat, add chopped chili, turmeric powder, and asafetida.
6. Mix seasoning and the lemon and salt mixture into rice. Cover and keep it on the counter for at least 2 hours before serving.
7. Serve rice at room temperature.

CHAPTER 3
SEASONING with HOT GHEE
Ghee ka Chounk

The sizzling sound of *chounk* coming from my

mother's kitchen told us that lunchtime was approaching. The mouth-watering aroma of ghee, roasted cumin seeds, and chilies filled the air as we waited anxiously for the call that lunch was ready. When I was about five years old, I was so fascinated by the daily ritual of making *chounk* that one of our elderly neighbors often sent for me before she started to season her dal. I loved to watch it bubble and hear the sputtering sound as the *chounk* mingled with the simmering lentils.

Several combinations of spices make different types of *chounk*. Among the most common and simple is the combination of whole cumin seeds with chili powder and asafetida. In northern India, these spices are also found in combination with ginger, garlic, onions, and tomatoes. In eastern India, whole spices such as cloves, cardamom, bay leaves, nigella seeds, and fennel seeds may be included. In southern India, mustard seeds, *chana* dal, *urad* dal, red chilies, and fresh curry leaves are used for seasoning.

Seasoning with *chounk* is one of the basic techniques in Indian cooking to enhance the taste of beans and legumes, commonly known as dal. Here I will introduce ghee (clarified butter) as the cooking medium. (In Chapter 2, I used oil as the medium.)

When ghee is used in *chounk*, you need fewer spices to prepare the seasoning. Upon heating, ghee gives off a distinct and pleasant aroma. *Chounk* made with hot ghee is mainly used to season lentils, which are mild in taste. Some vegetable and rice dishes such as *khichri* and vegetable *pullav* become aromatic and full of flavor when seasoned with hot ghee instead of hot oil.

Ghee is the clarified form of butter and can easily be prepared at home (see Chapter 7, page 164). It is also available in the ethnic section of grocery stores and in many Asian and Indian stores. Ghee can be heated to higher temperatures than butter without burning. It also has a much longer shelf life.

You can store ghee for about two to three months at room temperature. For longer storage, refrigerate or freeze it up to six to eight months. At room temperature, ghee is usually in a semiliquid state; at colder temperatures, it solidifies. When heated, ghee melts and changes to liquid form. In the recipes, ghee is measured in its liquid form;

therefore, it is important to melt the ghee before measuring.

Ghee is a common and integral ingredient in Indian cooking throughout the regions of India. Its use dates back to as early as 1500 B.C.—the Vedic period, known as the dawn of Indian civilization and a time when sacred Hindu hymns and prayers were compiled. For centuries, ghee has been used for religious ceremonies, for medicinal purposes in *Ayurvedic* medicine, and in everyday cooking.

Today, however, with a better awareness of healthy lifestyles, many people have reduced their ghee consumption. We know now that ghee is high in saturated fat and should be used in moderation. Regular vegetable cooking oil is often substituted or used in combination with ghee. It would, in my opinion, be sad to completely eliminate this tasty and flavorful ingredient from Indian cuisine. Fortunately, because of its distinct flavor and taste, even a small amount of ghee adds a wonderful aroma to a dish.

Using hot ghee seasoning

To season lentils: Cook the lentils separately (see Chapter 7, page 156), then temper them with the hot ghee seasoning. For lentils, you might make the ghee seasoning with fewer spices in order to maintain the simplicity and original taste of the lentils. To give lentils more intricate taste and texture, use fresh ingredients such as onions, tomatoes, and garlic along with the required spices in the seasoning.

Adding *chounk* to lentils not only enhances the taste and flavor but also has health benefits. Using fresh ingredients (such as ginger, garlic, and onions) and spices (such as asafetida) improves the digestibility of lentils and reduces the intestinal discomfort associated with eating beans and lentils.

To season rice and vegetables: Prepare the hot ghee seasoning first. Then cook the rice and vegetables with the seasoning.

You also use ghee to enhance food in ways besides

OBSERVATIONS and Helpful Tips

- Have all the required ingredients ready for use.

- Melt ghee beforehand to ensure that you use the required amount.

- Take care when handling chilies. Remove seeds from the chilies to reduce their potency.

- Have the lid to the pan handy. Cover when preparing the seasoning to avoid splattering and retain the flavor of the seasoning.

Most of the recipes in this chapter use only the six essential spices. By varying the spices and using additional spices of your choice, you can achieve a distinct flavor in each dish and maybe even create your own family and regional specialty.

The following spices and fresh ingredients are used in this chapter for preparing *chounk*.

Spices	Fresh Ingredients
Asafetida	Garlic
Cumin seeds	Ginger
Mustard seeds	Green chilies
Red chili powder	Lemon
Turmeric	Onion
Whole dry chilies	Tomato

preparing seasoning. Try drizzling ghee over plain rice or breads before serving. This final touch adds extra flavor and a distinct smell. Ghee is also a delicious ingredient used in a variety of sweets; it cannot be substituted without compromising taste.

Preparing *chounk* with ghee

To prepare *chounk* for lentils, use a small covered frying pan or a saucepan. To cook the vegetable dishes, use a covered, shallow frying pan large enough to hold the specified quantity of vegetables. To prepare rice dishes, make the seasoning in a covered, wide-bottomed, deep pan that allows space for the rice to expand.

Have all the necessary ingredients ready when you begin to prepare *chounk*. Place pan on the stove with the required amount of ghee at medium-high heat. Watch for overheating (the edges of ghee will start to turn brown and the ghee will start to smoke). If ghee overheats, remove pan from the heat and let it cool down before adding spices. To check if the ghee is hot enough, drop a few grains of the whole spices you are using (such as cumin or mustard seeds) into the hot ghee. The seeds should sizzle and come to the surface right away. If this does not happen, wait a few seconds and try again. Once the ghee is hot enough, you can start to make *chounk*.

Generally, we add dry, whole spices to the hot ghee first because they need the hottest temperature to release their flavors. After adding the spices, reduce the heat to medium and add the fresh ingredients (such as onions, ginger, garlic, and fresh chilies). Fry these ingredients lightly until they become soft. Add powdered spices (such as chili powder and asafetida) last to avoid burning or scorching them. This sequence is important. If not followed certain ingredients will be overcooked or undercooked. Chopped tomatoes are added to the seasoning as the last ingredient.

Pour the seasoning over the cooked lentils. Simmer lentils with seasoning for 10 minutes to achieve a thick, soup-like consistency. For rice and vegetable dishes, add uncooked rice or vegetables to the seasoning. Stir them into the prepared *chounk* and mix well. Continue cooking until seasoned rice or vegetables are done.

RECIPES

Brown Lentils
Masoor Dal

Brown lentils, or masoor *dal as they are known in northern India, are often cooked to a thick, soup-like consistency to get the best taste. Rice seasoned with cumin seeds or* tandoori roti *complements this dish best.*

INGREDIENTS
1 cup brown lentils, washed
4 to 5 cups water
$1/2$ teaspoon turmeric powder
1 teaspoon salt or to taste

SEASONING
2 tablespoons ghee
$1/2$ teaspoon cumin seeds
1 green chili, cut lengthwise
1 small onion (about $1/2$ cup chopped)
$1/4$ teaspoon red chili powder
1 medium tomato, chopped
2 to 3 tablespoons fresh lemon juice
$1/4$ cup cilantro, chopped

METHOD
1. Place lentils, water, turmeric powder, and salt in a medium-size saucepan. Bring to a boil on a high heat; reduce heat and cover the pan. Let simmer until lentils are soft and turn into a soup-like consistency. (You can also use a pressure cooker or slow cooker to cook the lentils. See Chapter 7, page 156.)
2. In a small frying pan, heat ghee on medium heat. When hot, stir cumin seeds into hot ghee. Add green chilies and onions. Cook until onions become soft.
3. Add red chili powder and tomatoes. Cook tomatoes until they become soft.
4. Add this seasoning to cooked lentils. Simmer lentils for another 10 minutes. Add lemon juice and garnish with cilantro.
5. Serve lentils hot.

Black-Eyed Peas
Lobia

In my kitchen, I make black-eyed peas (lobia) with a thick, soup-like consistency seasoned with hot ghee chunk *to serve with rice. Another way to prepare frozen black-eyed peas is to season them with hot oil* chunk, *using oil as the cooking medium. Garnish with fresh cilantro and chopped green chilies. Serve them hot with freshly squeezed lemon juice. This recipe makes a great afternoon snack.*

INGREDIENTS
- 1 cup black-eyed peas
- 4 cups water
- 1/2 teaspoon turmeric powder
- 1 teaspoon salt or to taste

SEASONING
- 2 tablespoons ghee
- 1/2 teaspoon cumin seeds
- 1 green chili, cut lengthwise and seeds removed
- 1 small onion (about 1/2 cup chopped)
- 1/2 teaspoon red chili powder
- 1 medium tomato, chopped
- 2 to 3 tablespoons fresh lemon juice
- 2 teaspoons sugar
- 1/4 cup cilantro, chopped

METHOD
1. Wash and soak the peas overnight—or at least 8 to 10 hours beforehand—to facilitate the cooking.
2. Drain water and transfer peas to a medium-size saucepan. Add the water, turmeric powder, and salt.
3. Bring to a boil on a high heat; reduce heat and cover the pan. Let simmer until peas are soft and turn into a soup-like consistency. (You can also use a pressure cooker or slow cooker to cook the peas. See Chapter 7, page 156.)
4. In a small frying pan, heat ghee on medium heat. When hot, stir cumin seeds into hot ghee.
5. Add green chilies and onions. Cook until onions become soft.
6. Stir in red chili powder and add tomatoes. Cook for another 3 to 4 minutes until tomatoes are soft.
7. Add this seasoning to cooked peas and simmer the peas for 10 minutes. Add lemon juice and sugar.
8. Garnish with fresh cilantro and serve hot.

Yellow Split Lentils and Spinach
Palak Dhuli Moong Dal

Dhuli moong *dal is a split and washed (without skin) variety of mung* (moong) *bean. These lentils are a light yellow color and oblong. This light lentil dish is easy to digest. To retain the original taste of the lentils, it's seasoned with few spices and often served with hot chapatis.*

INGREDIENTS
1 cup yellow split lentils *(dhuli moong* dal), washed
4 cups water
$1/2$ teaspoon turmeric powder
1 teaspoon salt or to taste
2 cups spinach, chopped
1 medium tomato, chopped
2 to 3 tablespoons fresh lemon juice

SEASONING
2 tablespoons ghee
$1/2$ teaspoon cumin seeds
2 whole red chilies
$1/2$ teaspoon red chili powder
$1/4$ teaspoon asafetida

METHOD
1. Place lentils in a saucepan with the water, turmeric powder, and salt. Bring to a boil on a high heat. Remove froth as it builds up. Adjust heat to keep from boiling over.
2. After frothing settles down, turn down heat to low. Cover the saucepan leaving a gap between the lid and pan to prevent froth formation and boiling over. Cook lentils until they are soft and turn into a soup-like consistency, about 15 to 20 minutes.
3. Add spinach and tomatoes; cook for another 10 minutes. Add lemon juice and remove from the heat.
4. In a small frying pan, heat ghee on medium heat. When hot, add cumin seeds and whole red chilies to ghee; fry them for few seconds. Remove pan from the stove.
5. Add red chili powder and asafetida. Pour the seasoning over the cooked lentils.
6. Serve hot with bread or rice. Or serve lentils as a soup.

Red Lentils
Lal Dal

Red lentils (lal dal) are a split and washed variety of brown lentils. They take less time to cook than brown ones. Red lentils have a distinct flavor and texture all their own.

INGREDIENTS
1 cup red lentils, washed
4 cups water
1/2 teaspoon turmeric powder
1 teaspoon salt or to taste

SEASONING
2 tablespoons ghee
1/2 teaspoon cumin seeds
1 green chili, cut lengthwise
1 small onion, chopped
1/2 teaspoon red chili powder
1 medium tomato, chopped
2 to 3 tablespoons fresh lemon juice
1/4 cup fresh cilantro, chopped

METHOD
1. Place lentils in a medium-size saucepan with the water, turmeric powder, and salt. Bring to a boil on a high heat. Reduce heat as froth starts to build up. Remove froth from the surface as it builds up.
2. After frothing settles down, turn down heat to low. Cover the saucepan leaving a gap between the lid and pan to prevent froth formation and boiling over.
3. Cook lentils until they are soft and turn into a soup-like consistency, about 15 to 20 minutes.
4. In a small frying pan, heat ghee on medium heat. When hot, add cumin seeds to ghee, soon followed by the green chilies and onions. Cook until onions become soft.
5. Add red chili powder and tomatoes. Cook for another 3 to 4 minutes until tomatoes become soft.
6. Add this seasoning to cooked lentils and simmer for another 10 minutes.
7. Add lemon juice, garnish with fresh cilantro, and serve hot.

SIX SPICES: A Simple Concept of Indian Cooking

Pigeon Peas
Tuar Dal

The creamy taste and mild flavor of tuar dal *makes this dish one of the most popular varieties of dal among kids and some fussy adult eaters. A more complex variation of* tuar dal *is* sambhar, *a dish from southern India.*

INGREDIENTS
1 cup pigeon peas (*tuar* dal)
4 cups water
1/2 teaspoon turmeric powder
1 teaspoon salt or to taste

SEASONING
2 tablespoons ghee
1/2 teaspoon cumin seeds
1/4 teaspoon red chili powder
1/4 teaspoon asafetida
1/4 cup tomato sauce or 1 cup chopped tomatoes
2 tablespoons fresh cilantro, chopped

METHOD
1. Wash peas in cold water, carefully discarding water each time until water becomes clear.
2. Place peas in a saucepan with the 4 cups of water, turmeric powder, and salt. Bring to a boil on a high heat. Reduce heat as froth starts to build up. Remove froth from the surface.
3. Turn heat to low and cover the saucepan, leaving a gap between the lid and pan to prevent froth formation and boiling over. Cook until peas are soft and turn into a soup-like consistency, about 30 to 40 minutes. (You can also use a pressure cooker or slow cooker to cook the peas. See Chapter 7, page 156.)
4. In a small frying pan, heat ghee on medium heat. When hot, add cumin seeds to ghee and reduce heat. Add red chili powder and asafetida.
5. Stir in tomato sauce or add chopped tomatoes to the seasoned ghee. Let sauce simmer for about 1 minute, or until tomatoes become soft.
6. Pour this seasoning over the cooked peas and simmer for another 10 minutes.
7. Garnish dish with fresh cilantro and serve it hot.

Spicy Pigeon Peas with Mixed Vegetables
Sambhar

Sambhar is a rich-tasting dish made of pigeon peas, vegetables, and a complex mixture of spices. It's normally served with rice dumplings for breakfast in southern India. When served with boiled rice, sambhar makes a complete and satisfying meal.

INGREDIENTS

1 cup pigeon peas (*tuar* dal)
4 cups water
1/2 teaspoon turmeric powder
1 teaspoon salt
2 tablespoons oil
1/2 teaspoon black mustard seeds
1/4 teaspoon red chili powder
1/8 teaspoon asafetida
5 to 6 fresh curry leaves (optional)
1 small onion, sliced
1 Asian eggplant, cut into 1-inch pieces
1 cup frozen Italian-style mixed vegetables
1 cup water, divided
1 teaspoon salt
1 tablespoon tamarind pulp (See Chapter 7, page 167)

SEASONING

2 tablespoons ghee
1/4 teaspoon cumin seeds
2 teaspoons coriander seeds
1/2 teaspoon urad dal
1/2 teaspoon chana dal
2 to 3 dry red chilies
1/4 cup fresh coconut, grated (See Chapter 7, page 160)
1/4 cup water

METHOD

1. Wash peas several times in cold water, carefully discarding water each time until water becomes clear.

2. Place peas in a saucepan with 4 cups of water, turmeric powder, and salt. Bring to a boil on a high heat. Reduce heat as froth starts to build up. Remove the froth from the surface.
3. Turn down heat to low and cover the saucepan, leaving a gap between the lid and pan to prevent froth formation and boiling over. Cook until peas are soft and turn into a soup-like consistency, about 30 to 40 minutes. (You can also use a pressure cooker or slow cooker to cook the peas. See Chapter 7, page 156.)
4. In a medium-size saucepan, heat 2 tablespoons of oil. When oil is hot, add mustard seeds and cover the pan until mustard seeds stop popping.
5. Remove pan from heat. Add red chili powder, asafetida, and curry leaves to hot oil. Cover pan to avoid splattering.
6. Return pan to stove and add onions and eggplant. Fry on medium heat for 5 minutes. Add the rest of the vegetables with 1/2 cup of water and salt. Cook vegetables until tender.
7. Mix tamarind pulp with 1/4 cup of remaining 1/2 cup of water to make a smooth paste. Add this paste to the cooked vegetables. Cook for another 5 minutes.
8. Place cooked peas and vegetables in a large pot. Simmer on low heat.
9. In a small frying pan, heat ghee. When hot, add cumin seeds, coriander seeds, and urad and chana dal. Fry until the dal become light brown in color. Add dry red chilies and fry another 30 seconds. Remove pan from the heat and mix in coconut.
10. Place this mixture in a blender and add remaining 1/4 cup of water. Run blender to grind the mixture into a fine paste. Add seasoning paste to the peas and vegetable mixture. Simmer for another 10 minutes.
11. Serve sambhar hot.

Rice and Yellow Split Lentil Porridge
Khichri

Vegetables add to the color and nutritional value of this version of khichri. *The use of* dhuli moong *dal in* khichri *makes it easy to digest.*

INGREDIENTS
1 cup long grain rice
3/4 cup yellow split lentils (*dhuli moong* dal)
2 tablespoons ghee
1/2 teaspoon cumin seeds
1 small onion, sliced
1/2 cup frozen peas
1/2 cup carrots, sliced
1/2 teaspoon turmeric powder
1 1/2 teaspoons salt or to taste
5 cups water

METHOD
1. Wash rice and lentils with cold water. Soak for 15 minutes before cooking.
2. Drain and discard the water. Set aside soaked rice and lentils.
3. Heat ghee in a large saucepan on medium-high heat. When hot, add cumin seeds to ghee and fry for 10 seconds.
4. Add onions; fry for 1 or 2 minutes, until onions become golden brown. Add peas and carrots; fry for another minute.
5. Add drained rice and lentils, turmeric powder, and salt to onion mixture. Fry until most of the water evaporates.
6. Add the 5 cups of water and bring to a boil on medium-high heat.
7. Reduce heat to medium-low. Partially cover pan with the lid, leaving a gap to prevent boiling over.
8. Simmer for 25 to 30 minutes, stirring occasionally until it turns into a porridge-like consistency.
9. Serve hot with plain yogurt, Indian pickles, and roasted or fried lentil wafers (*pappadum*).

Spicy Corn Kernels
Chounki Makka

Spicy corn kernels are a quick and popular snack for my family. A variation is prepared using frozen green peas. This recipe also makes a good side dish.

INGREDIENTS
1 10-ounce package frozen corn
2 teaspoons ghee
1/2 teaspoon cumin seeds
1 fresh green chili, chopped
1/4 teaspoon red chili powder
1/2 teaspoon salt or to taste
2 teaspoons fresh lemon juice
2 tablespoons fresh cilantro, chopped

METHOD
1. Do not thaw corn. Using frozen corn helps to cut down moisture during the cooking.
2. Heat ghee in a medium-size frying pan. When hot, add cumin seeds to ghee and reduce heat to medium. Add green chili and red chili powder.
3. Add corn; stir with spices. Add salt and cook until corn become soft and most of the moisture has evaporated, about 5 to 10 minutes.
4. Add lemon juice and garnish with chopped cilantro.
5. Serve hot as a snack or side dish.

Curried Potatoes
Aalu ki Subji

Potatoes are a versatile vegetable. A little change in spices and seasoning easily creates a new dish. Every household has its own unique way of preparing potato dishes. This dish is often served with puri, a deep-fried Indian bread.

INGREDIENTS
4 large potatoes (about 2 pounds)
3 tablespoons ghee
1 teaspoon cumin seeds
1 medium onion, chopped
1/2 teaspoon ginger, minced
1/4 teaspoon garlic, minced
1/4 teaspoon red chili powder
1 teaspoon salt or to taste
1 large tomato, chopped
2 tablespoons fresh cilantro, chopped

METHOD
1. Boil and cut potatoes into 1/2-inch cubes.
2. Heat ghee in a heavy frying pan. When hot, add cumin seeds to ghee and reduce heat to medium. Add onions, ginger, and garlic; fry until onions become soft. Add red chili powder and cook for another 30 seconds.
3. Add potatoes and salt. Stir the mixture until potatoes are coated with the spices.
4. Cover pan and reduce heat to medium-high. Cook for 5 to 10 minutes, stirring occasionally to avoid burning.
5. Add chopped tomato and cook for another minute or two. Remove from heat.
6. Garnish with freshly chopped cilantro.
7. Serve potatoes hot.

Rice Pilaf with Mixed Vegetables
Subji ka Chawal

The combination of rice with vegetables makes this a complete meal. It can be served with yogurt, chicken curry, or chole *(garbanzo beans). This recipe is an excellent picnic dish because it doesn't spoil easily.*

INGREDIENTS

    1 cup basmati rice or long grain rice
    2 tablespoons ghee
    1/2 teaspoon cumin seeds
    2 whole red chilies
    1 teaspoon whole coriander seeds, crushed
    1 medium onion, sliced
    2 cups assorted frozen or fresh vegetables
    1 teaspoon salt or to taste
    2 cups water

METHOD

1. Wash rice with cold water and soak for 15 minutes before cooking.
2. Heat ghee in medium-size saucepan on low heat. When hot, add cumin seeds to ghee and fry for 10 seconds. Add red chilies and crushed coriander seeds.
3. Add onions and cook until soft. Add vegetables and fry for 2 minutes.
4. Drain water from the rice. Add drained rice and salt to the vegetables. Fry for another 1 or 2 minutes until most of the moisture evaporates.
5. Add the 2 cups of water and bring to a boil on medium-high heat. Reduce heat to medium-low and cook rice for 10 to 15 minutes.
6. Fluff rice with a fork and empty onto a large platter. Loosely cover with foil and let stand for 10 minutes.
7. Serve rice hot or at room temperature.

Egg and Tomato Scramble
Bhurji

Egg bhurji *is a common winter breakfast in India, served with hot toast or* paratha *(pan-fried bread) prepared on an iron griddle. Red tomatoes, green cilantro, and purple onions add color.*

INGREDIENTS
4 to 5 large eggs
1/4 cup onion, chopped
1 green chili, chopped
1 small tomato, chopped
2 tablespoons fresh cilantro, chopped
1/4 teaspoon red chili powder
1/2 teaspoon salt or to taste
3 tablespoons ghee
1 teaspoon cumin seeds

METHOD
1. In a large glass bowl, break eggs and beat them lightly.
2. Stir onions, green chilies, tomatoes, cilantro, red chili powder, and salt into eggs.
3. Heat ghee in a medium-size, nonstick frying pan on medium to high heat. When hot, add cumin seeds to ghee and reduce heat to medium.
4. Pour egg mixture into pan and cook until eggs start to set. Stir the mixture to scramble.
5. Cook thoroughly, stirring the egg mixture occasionally.
6. Serve hot with bread.

Potatoes with Cumin Seeds
Jeere ke Aalu

Potatoes with cumin seeds are a quick and easy way to spice up your regular Sunday brunch. They also make a great side dish to complement an Indian meal when served with puri (deep-fried Indian bread).

INGREDIENTS

3 tablespoons ghee
1/2 teaspoon cumin seeds
1/4 teaspoon red chili powder
1/4 teaspoon asafetida
1 16-ounce package frozen Southern-style hash browns or 4 large potatoes, boiled, peeled, and cut into 1/4-inch pieces
1 teaspoon salt or to taste
3/4 teaspoon cumin powder

METHOD

1. Heat ghee in a heavy, medium-size frying pan. When hot, add cumin seeds to ghee and fry for 10 seconds.
2. Remove pan from heat. Stir in red chili powder and asafetida.
3. Add hash browns or potatoes and salt. Stir the mixture until hash browns or potatoes are coated with spices.
4. Cover pan and reduce heat to medium. Cook for 5 to 10 minutes, stirring occasionally until potatoes are golden brown.
5. Sprinkle with cumin powder.
6. Serve hot or at room temperature as a side dish.

Saffron Rice

Kesar Chawal

When served with meat curries, saffron rice enhances the curries and brings out their wonderful aromas. Saffron rice makes a fragrant and satisfying accompaniment to dishes served at special gatherings.

INGREDIENTS
1 cup basmati rice
1/4 teaspoon saffron
3 tablespoons ghee
1/2 teaspoon cumin seeds
2 cups water
1 teaspoon salt or taste

METHOD
1. Wash rice with cold water and soak for 15 minutes before cooking.
2. Soak saffron in 2 tablespoons of warm water.
3. In medium saucepan, heat ghee on medium heat. When hot, add cumin seeds to ghee and fry for 10 seconds.
4. Drain and discard water from the rice. Add drained rice to seasoned ghee. Fry until most of the water evaporates.
5. Add the 2 cups of water and bring to a boil on medium-high heat. Add soaked saffron with soaking water. Add salt. Cover the pan, leaving a small gap between pan and lid. Reduce heat to medium-low. Cook rice for 10 to 15 minutes. Watch carefully to prevent boiling over.
6. Fluff rice with a fork and empty onto a large platter. Loosely cover with foil and let stand for 10 minutes. You may garnish rice with thinly sliced fried onions.
7. Serve rice hot.

Rice with Cumin Seeds

Jeere ke Chawal

Ghee and cumin seeds give rice an amazing taste, making cumin rice the simplest version of flavorful rice dishes. This is a wonderful complementary dish for rajma *(kidney beans) and* kadhi *(chickpea flour dumpling in yogurt sauce).*

INGREDIENTS
1 cup basmati rice
2 tablespoons ghee
$^{1}/_{2}$ teaspoon cumin seeds
2 cups water
1 teaspoon salt or to taste

METHOD
1. Wash rice with cold water and soak for 15 minutes before cooking.
2. Heat ghee in medium-size saucepan on medium heat. When hot, add cumin seeds to ghee and fry for 10 seconds.
3. Drain and discard water from the rice. Add drained rice to seasoned ghee. Fry until most of the water evaporates.
4. Add the 2 cups of water and the salt. Bring to a boil on medium-high heat. Reduce heat to medium-low and cook rice for 10 to 15 minutes. Watch carefully to prevent boiling over.
5. Fluff rice with a fork and empty onto a large platter. Loosely cover with foil and let stand for 10 minutes.
6. Serve rice hot.

CHAPTER 4
COOKING with POWDERED SPICES
Sookha Masala

The day we saw the red chili peppers, brown

coriander seeds, and yellow roots of turmeric drying in the sun, we knew what awaited.

Gharrrrr, gharrrrr, gharrrr. The sound of a *chakki* (grinding stone) and the thumps of a *hamam dasta* (mortar and pestle) kept us away from the courtyard of our home, where the air was pungent and strong. We made sure we stayed clear of the activities, taking the opportunity to have fun outdoors and visit our friends in their homes. The grinding and pounding was a yearly ritual as winter ended and summer began. It was the season when the spice crops were ready to be pounded and ground into powdered spices.

The task was left to the professionals. The women worked in pairs, carrying their grinding stones and other required supplies from home to home throughout the neighborhood. The spices had to be dried, ground, sifted, and stored with great care at each step. Today this wonderful ritual has been replaced by modern machines. Prepackaged powdered spices are available at the local *kirana* stores that also sell other grocery items for everyday use.

Asafetida, chili, turmeric, coriander, and cumin are the basic powdered spices used daily in Indian cooking to prepare an assortment of vegetable and meat recipes. In this chapter, my emphasis is on using powdered spices to create a variety of vegetable dishes.

Besides the basic individual powdered spices, spice mixes such as garam masala, *sambhar masala,* and *chat masala* are used in regional cooking to give a distinct taste to a particular dish. Most of these mixes are now available at Indian stores, but you can make them at home using precise amounts of spices to attain a particular taste. Sometimes, to achieve a unique flavor in a dish, you will want to first roast the whole spices and then powder them. The roasted powder is best when prepared just before using.

Spices are used in different forms. For example, cumin and coriander seeds are added whole to season the oil. You can use a powdered form of cumin and coriander seeds for extra flavor and to thicken the gravy. Roasted and powdered cumin and coriander seeds give a strong and roasted flavor. Similarly, you can use chilies whole, crushed, or powdered. Each form adds varying degrees of spiciness to a dish.

By using different ways to incorporate the spices into a dish, you will greatly influence the taste, texture, and appearance of each preparation. You will be able to cook some vegetable dishes just by using a few spices. Other dishes may require elaborate techniques involving several steps and a number of spices. One recipe may call for cooking vegetables until they are barely tender, but others may require vegetables to be simmered in the spicy sauce until well seasoned. Slow simmering gives the vegetables a chance to absorb the full flavor of the spices.

You can prepare vegetables with powdered spices in three ways: vegetables without gravy (*sookhi subji*), vegetables with a light gravy (*rase ki subji*), or as stuffed vegetables (*bharvan subji*).

Preparing vegetables using powdered spices

Select vegetables, wash them, and peel if required. Cut vegetables into about the same size pieces, which helps cook them evenly. For stuffed preparation, select vegetables similar in size for uniform cooking. Wash and dry vegetables before stuffing.

Method One: **Vegetables without gravy.** This is the simplest way to prepare a vegetable dish. It is a slight variation of the hot oil seasoning (*tel ka chounk*). In addition to the spices used in *chounk,* coriander and cumin powders are used.

You should have all the ingredients ready before you begin to cook. Choose a nonstick frying pan of appropriate size so vegetables can be turned frequently and stirred with ease. If the pan is too small, it will be difficult to stir the contents and the spices and vegetables will not mix well. If the pan is too large, the vegetables burn very easily.

Heat the required amount of oil on high-to-medium heat in the pan. To check the temperature, drop a few mustard or cumin seeds into the hot oil. The seeds should sizzle and come to surface of the oil; if not, wait a few more seconds and repeat.

OBSERVATIONS and Helpful Tips

- For the first two methods, cut the vegetables into approximately the same size pieces to ensure that all the pieces will cook in just about the same time.

- For the first two methods, stir-fry vegetables for two to three minutes in a small amount of oil to help keep them firm but tender until the end of the cooking.

- Select the same size vegetables for making stuffed vegetables.

- Use a nonstick pan to keep the amount of oil required to a minimum.

When mustard seeds are used in a recipe, always add them first to the hot oil. Follow with the other whole spices, such as cumin seeds. This sequence gives the mustard seeds a chance to cook and release their full flavor. Be sure to cover the pan immediately after adding the mustard seeds to prevent them from splattering; keep the pan covered until the seeds stop popping.

After adding whole spices, reduce heat to medium and add fresh ingredients such as chopped ginger or garlic. Let them sizzle in the hot oil to release their flavors, taking care not to burn them. Depending on the recipe, add turmeric and chili powder to the hot oil. Coriander and cumin powder can be added at this time or as the recipe instructs. Stir the spices in the hot oil for few seconds and add the vegetables to the spice mixture. Mix well to coat all the vegetable pieces evenly with the spice mixture. Add salt and cook the vegetables with the spices on medium heat.

Adjust the cooking temperature as needed, depending on the amount of juices released by the vegetables during cooking.

Some varieties of vegetables do not always release enough moisture when heated. To keep these vegetables moist and tender, it is important to reduce the heat to medium-to-low and keep the pan covered. You may need an additional sprinkle of water to keep sufficient moisture in the pan.

Other vegetables release more than enough juices. To reduce excess moisture after vegetables are tender and soft, uncover the pan and increase the heat to medium-high. Stir vegetables occasionally to reduce the chance of burning or scorching. Cook until desired amount of moisture or juice is left. Turn off the heat and remove the pan.

Method Two: **Vegetables with a light gravy.** This method involves making a smooth paste with the required powdered spices. The paste is gently roasted in oil on medium-low heat to achieve a fragrant spice mixture.

Generally, you will not use whole spices such as mustard and cumin seeds to prepare vegetables with a light gravy. You will use powdered spices such as turmeric, chili, cumin, and coriander along with ginger, onion, and garlic as fresh ingredients. To cook the vegetables, simmer them in the spice mixture. The final product usually has a small amount of gravy.

Before you begin to make the paste, you should have all the ingredients ready. Place the required powdered spices in a small bowl and add a small amount of warm water (just enough to make a smooth paste). The paste will have the consistency of apple sauce.

Heat the required amount of oil in a nonstick frying pan on medium-high heat. Make sure to choose a pan of the appropriate size. When the oil is hot enough, add chopped fresh ingredients. To check the temperature, drop a few pieces of chopped onion or garlic into the hot oil; they should sizzle right away. Reduce the heat to medium and cook the fresh ingredients until they are soft and translucent, stirring occasionally to prevent burning.

The following list includes the main spices and fresh ingredients used to cook the vegetables in this chapter.

Spices	Fresh Ingredients
Asafetida	Cilantro
Coriander seeds and powder	Green chilies
Cumin seeds and powder	Garlic
Mustard seeds	Ginger
Red chili powder	Onion
Turmeric powder	Tomato

Stir in the spice paste and reduce the heat to medium-to-low. Continue to cook, stirring in a spoonful of water at a time (the required amount is given in the recipes). Add more water as needed to prevent burning the paste. After adding water and cooking for a while, the oil will begin to separate from the spice mixture. At this time, the raw smell of spices and fresh ingredients changes into a roasted and fragrant smell. Add the vegetables and salt according to the recipe and stir well into the spice mixture. A light gravy is created with the moisture released by the vegetables during cooking or with the water you've added. Cover the pan and let the vegetables simmer in this gravy until they are tender and well seasoned with the spices.

Method Three: **Stuffed vegetables.** For this method, you should select small and tender vegetables. Wash and dry them to prepare for stuffing. Prepare round vegetables such as tomatoes, bell peppers, and potatoes by cutting a square opening at one end and scooping out the insides. For thin and long vegetables such as okra, banana pepper, and bitter gourd, slit the vegetables lengthwise and hollow out if needed.

Powdered spices and fresh ingredients are used to prepare the filling. Nuts, roasted chickpea flour, sesame seeds, fresh coconut, and boiled potatoes can also be used.

The stuffing or filling is prepared in two ways. In the first way, you simply mix powdered spices such as turmeric, chili, coriander, and salt in a bowl in certain proportions. You then fill individual vegetable pieces through the opening or the cut with the spice mixture.

The second way, which is more elaborate, requires several additional ingredients and preparation steps for the stuffing. Chop the fresh ingredients such as onion, ginger, and garlic and cook them in a little bit of oil on medium heat. Lightly fry them for a minute or two before adding the powdered spices. Cook this mixture by adding a little water at a time, until it becomes thick and smooth and has a roasted and appetizing smell. At this time, add the other ingredients such as nuts, coconut, boiled potatoes, or any other ingredients as called for in the recipe. Remove the pan from the heat and let the mixture cool. Divide into equal portions and fill each hollowed vegetable. Some vegetables may need to be secured either with a toothpick or by wrapping thread around each vegetable to hold the filling inside while it's cooking.

To cook the stuffed vegetables, heat oil in a nonstick frying pan on medium heat. If called for according to the recipe, add sliced onions and fry them for a minute or two. Add the stuffed vegetables and cover the pan. Cook on medium-to-low heat, turning them occasionally to brown all sides. Cooking time depends on the size and thickness of the vegetables. Check for tenderness by piercing the skin with a toothpick; the vegetable skin should pierce easily. Remove the pan from the heat when vegetables are tender yet firm. Keep them warm until serving.

RECIPES

Potatoes and Cauliflower Curry
Aalu Gobhi ki Subji

Cauliflower is available in abundance during the winter in India. It is often cooked in combination with potatoes or peas. It's simple and quick to cook, which makes it a popular curry in many households. By adding coriander powder toward the end of the cooking instead of tomatoes, one can create a dish with an entirely different taste.

INGREDIENTS
1 medium-size cauliflower
2 medium potatoes
3 tablespoons cooking oil
1/2 teaspoon cumin seeds
1 teaspoon fresh ginger, chopped
1/2 teaspoon red chili powder
1/4 teaspoon turmeric powder
1 teaspoon salt
1 medium-size ripe tomato, chopped
2 tablespoons fresh cilantro, chopped

METHOD
1. Wash and cut cauliflower into medium-size florets. Peel and cut potatoes into 1/2-inch cubes.
2. Heat oil on medium heat in a nonstick frying pan. Add cumin seeds to the hot oil and fry for a few seconds. Stir in ginger, chili powder, and turmeric powder. Reduce heat to medium-high.
3. Add cauliflower, potatoes, and salt. Mix them well so the vegetables are coated with spices. Cover and cook on medium heat, stirring occasionally.
4. When cooked (potatoes should easily break with slight pressure), add tomatoes. Cook another 2 minutes or until tomatoes become soft.
5. If necessary, on high heat, dry out any juices from the curry. Stir frequently but gently to keep vegetables from sticking to the pan and to avoid breaking the florets.
6. Sprinkle with cilantro and serve it hot.

Cabbage and Peas Curry
Patta-gobhi aur Matar ki Subji

This curry is a simple and a quick dish. It makes a delicious side dish to the main meal. For a unique taste, add powdered fennel seeds or chopped tomatoes toward the end of the cooking time.

INGREDIENTS
2 tablespoons cooking oil
1/2 teaspoon black mustard seeds
2 green chilies, sliced lengthwise
3/4 teaspoon turmeric powder
1/2 teaspoon red chili powder
1 cup frozen peas
6 to 7 cups cabbage, shredded
1 teaspoon salt
2 tablespoons fresh cilantro, chopped

METHOD
1. Heat oil in a large frying pan on medium-high heat. When oil is hot, add mustard seeds. Immediately cover the pan and remove from heat. When the popping stops, return pan to heat. Add green chilies, turmeric powder, and chili powder.
2. Stir in peas and cook for 2 minutes. Add cabbage and salt; mix well. Cover and cook on medium-high heat. Adjust heat if cabbage starts sticking to the pan.
3. When peas and cabbage are soft and most of the liquid has evaporated, remove pan from the heat.
4. Sprinkle with cilantro.
5. Serve hot or at room temperature.

Carrots and Peas Curry

Gajar Matar ki Subji

This sweet-and-sour dish goes well with any Indian bread. Replacing the lemon juice with dry mango powder as the souring agent will give this curry a tart taste. Dry mango powder is available at Indian food stores.

INGREDIENTS

2 tablespoons cooking oil
1 teaspoon black mustard seeds
3/4 teaspoon turmeric powder
1/2 teaspoon red chili powder
1 cup frozen peas
3 cups sliced carrots or 10-ounce package frozen carrots
1 teaspoon salt
2 tablespoons lemon juice
1 tablespoon coriander powder
2 teaspoons sugar

METHOD

1. Heat oil in a large frying pan on medium-high heat. When oil is hot, add mustard seeds. Immediately cover the pan and remove from heat. When popping stops, return pan to heat and stir in turmeric powder and chili powder.
2. Add peas and cook for 1 minute. Add carrots and salt; mix well. Cover the pan and cook on medium heat. Adjust heat if carrots start sticking to the pan.
3. When peas and carrots are cooked and soft to touch, add lemon juice, coriander powder, and sugar; mix well. Cover and cook for another 5 minutes.
4. Remove from the stove and let it stand for 10 minutes before serving.

Dry Curried Potatoes I

Sookhe Aalu I

This satisfying savory dish is full of flavor and taste. The potatoes can be served as a side to complete a meal or as a snack with hot tea or lassi. *This recipe is often a life-saver with the fussy eater and children.*

INGREDIENTS

4 large potatoes
3 tablespoons cooking oil
1 teaspoon cumin seeds
1/2 teaspoon red chili powder
1/4 teaspoon asafetida
1 teaspoon salt
1 tablespoon fresh lemon juice
2 tablespoons fresh cilantro, chopped

METHOD

1. Boil, peel, and cut potatoes to desired size cubes.
2. Heat oil in a heavy frying pan. When oil is hot, add cumin seeds and reduce heat to medium. Stir in chili powder and asafetida.
3. Add potatoes and salt. Stir the mixture so that potatoes are coated with spices.
4. Cover the pan and reduce heat to medium. Fry potatoes, turning often to keep them from sticking to pan. When golden brown, remove from heat.
5. Mix in lemon juice. Garnish with cilantro.
6. Serve potatoes hot.

Dry Curried Potatoes II
Sookhe Aalu II

In this potato curry, we use fresh ingredients along with powdered spices to give added flavor. Just four spices keeps the dish simple. These potatoes go well with puris (deep-fried bread) or paratha *(semi-fried bread) along with Indian pickles.*

INGREDIENTS

4 large potatoes
3 tablespoons cooking oil
1 teaspoon cumin seeds
1/2 teaspoon ginger, minced
1/2 teaspoon garlic, minced
1/4 teaspoon red chili powder
1/4 teaspoon turmeric powder
1 teaspoon salt
1 teaspoon coriander powder
1 teaspoon cumin powder
2 tablespoons fresh cilantro, chopped

METHOD

1. Peel and cut potatoes into 1/2-inch cubes.
2. Heat oil in a heavy saucepan. When oil is hot, add cumin seeds and reduce heat to medium. Add ginger and garlic; fry for 10 seconds. Stir in chili and turmeric powders.
3. Add potatoes and salt. Stir the mixture until potatoes are coated with spices.
4. Cover the pan and reduce heat to medium-high. Stir occasionally until potatoes are cooked.
5. Sprinkle with coriander and cumin powder. Cook uncovered for another 5 minutes, turning occasionally to keep potatoes from sticking to pan.
6. Garnish with cilantro.
7. Serve potatoes with hot Indian bread.

Curried Zucchini

Zucchini ki Subji

Zucchini is one of my favorite vegetables. It can be prepared in so many different ways. By making simple changes in the spices and also by altering cooking techniques, I create a completely different taste. Zucchini can also be cooked in combination with other vegetables, such as bell peppers, onions, corn, and potatoes.

INGREDIENTS

3 tablespoons cooking oil
1 teaspoon black mustard seeds
1 small onion, chopped
3/4 teaspoon turmeric powder
1/2 teaspoon red chili powder
1 tablespoon coriander powder
1/4 cup water
5 cups zucchini, quartered lengthwise and cut into 1-inch pieces
1 teaspoon salt
2 tablespoons lemon juice
2 teaspoons sugar

METHOD

1. Heat oil in a large frying pan on medium-high heat. When oil is hot, add mustard seeds. Immediately cover the pan and remove from heat. When popping stops, return pan to heat.
2. Add onions and cook until soft. Reduce heat and add turmeric, chili, and coriander powders.
3. Gradually stir 1/4 cup water, 2 tablespoons at a time, into the spice mixture. Cook for 2 minutes until spices form a smooth paste.
4. Add zucchini. Stir until all pieces are coated with the spice mixture. Cover and cook for 10 minutes. Add salt and cook until zucchini is soft to the touch.
5. Add lemon juice and sugar.
6. Cook for another 2 minutes and serve hot.

Curried Zucchini in Peanut Sauce
Zucchini Moongfali ki Subji

Zucchini with peanut sauce goes well over boiled rice. It has a sweet-and-sour taste and a coarse texture. If you add a little more water at Step 8, you can have this curry with gravy.

INGREDIENTS

2 teaspoons coriander powder
1/2 teaspoon turmeric powder
1/2 teaspoon red chili powder
1/2 cup water
4 tablespoons oil, divided
1/4 teaspoon asafetida
2 pounds zucchini, quartered
   lengthwise and cut into 1-inch pieces

2 cloves garlic, chopped
3/4 cup onion, finely chopped
1 teaspoon salt
2 teaspoons sugar
1 tablespoon lemon juice
4 tablespoons crushed peanuts
   (See Chapter 7, page 165)

METHOD

1. In a small bowl, mix coriander, turmeric, and chili powders with 1/4 cup of the water to make paste. Set aside.
2. In a large nonstick frying pan, heat 1 tablespoon oil over medium to high heat.
3. When oil is hot, stir in asafetida. Add zucchini pieces and stir-fry for 5 minutes.
4. Remove pan from heat and transfer zucchini to a dish. Return pan to stove. Add remaining 3 tablespoons oil; heat oil on medium heat.
5. Add garlic and onions to hot oil and sauté until onions become soft and translucent.
6. Mix the coriander, turmeric, and chili paste into the onions and garlic. Reduce heat to medium and continue to cook, adding a spoonful of water at a time until all the remaining water is used up. At this stage, oil will separate from the onion mixture, and the raw smell of spices will change to a roasted and more flavorful smell.
7. Add zucchini and stir well to coat all pieces with the spices. Cover and cook for 5 minutes. Add salt and stir well. Cover the pan and cook for about 10 to 12 minutes or until zucchini is tender and cooked.
8. Add sugar, lemon juice, and peanuts. Stir to mix well with the zucchini. Cover the pan and cook for another 5 minutes on low heat.
9. Transfer to a serving dish. Serve hot with chapati or over boiled rice.

Stuffed Okra with Onions

Bharvan Bhindi Piyaz ke sath

This recipe is one of the simplest ways to make okra. In this recipe, I use fewer spices to retain the taste of the okra. Be sure to pick only small and tender pods for this dish.

INGREDIENTS
1 pound small and tender okra pods
1 small onion
3/4 teaspoon turmeric powder
1/2 teaspoon red chili powder
3 teaspoons coriander powder
1/2 teaspoon salt
2 to 3 tablespoons cooking oil
2 teaspoons lemon juice

METHOD
1. Wash and completely dry okra pods.
2. Remove the crown and tail from each pod and slit lengthwise.
3. Peel and slice onion lengthwise.
4. Mix turmeric, chili, and coriander powders, and salt in a small bowl. Divide mixture into an equal portion for each pod.
5. Take each pod, open the slit, and fill with the spice mixture.
6. Heat oil in a nonstick frying pan over medium heat. When oil is hot, add sliced onions and cook until wilted.
7. Add okra to onions; stir so okra pods are well coated with oil. Cover the pan and cook, stirring occasionally, until okra pods are soft and tender.
8. Sprinkle with lemon juice and toss okra gently to mix well.
9. Serve it hot with bread.

Eggplant and Mushroom Curry

Baingan Khumbhi ki Subji

Eggplant comes in many varieties. There are the long Asian eggplants; the small, round baby eggplants; and large, flashy eggplants. Each one has a distinct texture. Eggplant can also be cooked in combination with bell peppers, potatoes, and peas; each variation has its own taste.

INGREDIENTS

6 tablespoons cooking oil, divided
8 ounces sliced mushrooms
1 medium eggplant, cut into 1-inch cubes
1/2 teaspoon cumin seeds
1 small onion, chopped
2 cloves garlic, chopped
3/4 teaspoon turmeric powder
1/2 teaspoon red chili powder
1 tablespoon coriander powder
1/4 cup water
1 teaspoon salt
1 medium tomato, chopped
1/4 cup cilantro, chopped

METHOD

1. In a medium-size pan, heat 2 tablespoons of oil on medium heat. When oil is hot, add sliced mushrooms and eggplant. Stir-fry until vegetables start to turn brown, 5 to 6 minutes. Transfer to a plate.
2. Heat remaining oil in the same pan. When hot, add cumin seeds and stir for few seconds. Add onions and garlic. Cook until they become soft, stirring often to prevent burning.
3. Stir turmeric, chili, and coriander powders into the onions and garlic. Add 2 tablespoons of water at a time until all the water is used up and spices form a smooth paste.
4. Add mushrooms, eggplant, and salt. Stir well with the spices. Cover, stirring occasionally, until vegetables are cooked. Add tomatoes and cook for another 2 minutes.
5. Garnish with fresh cilantro and serve hot.

Vegetable Delight
Mili-Juli Subji

The variety of vegetables in this dish gives it an attractive texture and an assortment of colors and flavors. It is better to prepare this a day ahead for best results, so the vegetables have additional time to absorb the many flavors.

The recipe is divided into three steps. Each gives you the list of ingredients followed by detailed instructions for assembling the dish. You can make this with different combinations of vegetables.

STEP 1
1/2 teaspoon red chili powder
1/2 teaspoon turmeric powder
1/4 teaspoon paprika
2 tablespoons coriander powder
3 tablespoons warm water

Mix the spices in a bowl with the water to make a smooth paste. Set it aside to be used later.

STEP 2
3 tablespoons oil
1/2 teaspoon cumin seeds
1/4 teaspoon asafetida
2 cups cauliflower, cut into small florets
1 cup carrots, cut into 1/4-inch pieces
1 cup zucchini, cut lengthwise and then cut into 1-inch-long pieces
2 cups potatoes, peeled and cut into 1-inch cubes

In a large saucepan, heat oil on medium heat. When oil is hot, add cumin seeds and asafetida. Stir in all the vegetables. Fry for about 6 to 8 minutes.

STEP 3
6 tablespoons oil
1 cup onion, chopped
1 tablespoon fresh ginger, minced
1 tablespoon fresh garlic, minced
1 cup water

3/4 cup tomato sauce
1/2 cup yogurt
1 1/2 teaspoons salt or to taste
1/4 cup fresh cilantro, chopped

METHOD

1. Heat oil in a large saucepan over medium heat. When hot, add onions, ginger, and garlic. Fry until onions become soft.
2. Add spice paste from Step 1 to onion mixture; fry on low-to-medium heat. Add 2 to 3 tablespoons of water, one tablespoon at a time, until oil separates from the spice and onion mixture.
3. Add tomato sauce; cook until oil separates from the mixture. Add yogurt and salt; cook until it makes a smooth sauce.
4. Add vegetables from Step 2 to the sauce. Stir until all the pieces are coated well with sauce. Cover saucepan and turn heat to medium.
5. Cook for 10 minutes, stirring occasionally. Add 1 cup water to mixture; cover and turn heat to low. Cook for another 15 minutes or until vegetables are cooked and soft to the touch.
6. Garnish curry with cilantro. Serve hot.

Cucumber, Tomato, and Onion
with Yogurt

Kheere, Tamatar, Piyaz ka Raita

A yogurt dish known as raita *is often served with meals to offset spicy food. Fewer spices are used in* raita *to retain the natural taste and freshness of the vegetables.*

INGREDIENTS
2 cups plain yogurt
1 medium tomato, chopped
1 small cucumber, peeled and chopped
1 small onion, chopped
$1/2$ teaspoon roasted cumin powder, divided (See Chapter 7, page 161)
$1/2$ teaspoon salt or to taste
1 teaspoon sugar
$1/4$ teaspoon paprika

METHOD
1. Mix yogurt in a bowl until smooth.
2. Add tomatoes, cucumber, and onions.
3. Mix in $1/4$ teaspoon of the roasted cumin powder. Cover bowl and refrigerate *raita*.
4. Mix in salt and sugar just before serving. Place *raita* in serving dish.
5. Sprinkle with remaining $1/4$ teaspoon roasted cumin powder and paprika to give this plain-looking dish a festive look.
6. Serve *raita* cold or at room temperature.

Cucumber with Yogurt
Kheere ka Raita

Cucumber raita *makes a light and cool side dish for spicy dishes and summer meals. It can be prepared in just a few minutes.* Raita *also makes a great complementary dish for many rice preparations.*

INGREDENTS
2 cups plain yogurt
1 cup cucumber, peeled and grated
3/4 teaspoon salt
2 teaspoons sugar
1/2 teaspoon red chili powder
1/2 teaspoon roasted cumin powder (See Chapter 7, page 161)

METHOD
1. Mix yogurt in a bowl until smooth.
2. Remove excess water from cucumber by placing cucumber through a sieve. Discard liquid and mix cucumber with yogurt.
3. Add salt, sugar, chili powder, and roasted cumin powder. Mix well.
4. Refrigerate *raita* to keep it cool or serve it at room temperature.

Chicken in Peanut Sauce

Murgi Moongfali ke sath

This recipe is a very quick and simple way to prepare chicken. The sweet-and-sour tasting chicken with peanut sauce goes very well over boiled rice.

INGREDIENTS

2 teaspoons coriander powder
1/2 teaspoon turmeric powder
1/2 teaspoon red chili powder
3/4 cup water, divided
4 tablespoons oil
1 large onion, chopped very fine
2 pounds boneless, skinless chicken thighs or breasts, cut into 1-inch pieces
1 teaspoon salt
1 tablespoon lemon juice
2 teaspoons brown sugar
4 tablespoons crushed peanuts (See Chapter 7, page 165)

METHOD

1. In a small bowl, mix coriander, turmeric, and chili powders with 1/4 cup of the water to make a paste. Set it aside.
2. In a nonstick frying pan, heat oil. When oil is hot, add chopped onions and sauté until onions become soft and translucent.
3. Add spice paste. Reduce heat to medium and continue to cook, adding a tablespoon of 1/4 cup of water at a time. Repeat 2 to 3 times.
4. Add chicken to the above paste; stir well to coat all the pieces with the spices. Cook for 2 to 3 minutes.
5. Add salt and cook for another 5 minutes, stirring occasionally
6. Add lemon juice and the remaining 1/4 cup of water.
7. Add brown sugar and peanuts. Cook for another 5 to 10 minutes.
8. Transfer it to a serving dish. Serve it hot with chapati or boiled rice.

Stuffed Peppers

Bharvan Mirch

Stuffed vegetables are a treat since the cook takes extra time and special care to prepare them. Instead of cooking these stuffed peppers in a pan as called for in this recipe, you can bake them in the oven at 375°F for 20 minutes, or until they are soft to the touch. Turn the peppers once halfway through the baking so they cook evenly.

INGREDIENTS

8 to 10 small, tender bell peppers	1/2 teaspoon red chili powder
4 medium potatoes	1/2 teaspoon turmeric powder
4 tablespoons oil, divided	1 teaspoon coriander powder
1 small onion, chopped	2 tablespoons lemon juice
1 teaspoon salt	2 tablespoons fresh cilantro, chopped

METHOD

1. Wash and dry the bell peppers. To remove the seeds, use a sharp knife to cut around the stem of each pepper. Carefully remove the stems, saving them for later use.
2. With a small spoon, carefully remove the seeds from inside the peppers.
3. Boil the potatoes. When cooked, drain; peel after they have cooled down. Mash potatoes coarsely.
4. In nonstick frying pan, heat 2 tablespoons of oil on medium-high heat. When oil is hot, add chopped onions and sauté for 1 or 2 minutes.
5. When onions become light brown, reduce heat to medium and add mashed potatoes, salt, red chili, turmeric, and coriander powders, and lemon juice.
6. Cook potatoes for 5 minutes, stirring occasionally to mix the spices into the potatoes. Sprinkle with cilantro and cook for another 2 minutes. Remove the pan from the heat and let the mixture cool.
7. Divide the mixture into equal portions. Carefully place each portion into a pepper. Use the stem to cover the opening.
8. Heat the remaining oil in the same pan on medium heat. Place the stuffed peppers in the pan. Cover the pan and cook the peppers until they are browned on all sides and are soft to the touch (a toothpick should pierce it easily). Stir them occasionally to prevent burning and scorching. This step should be done just before serving them to keep peppers firm and tender.
9. Serve peppers hot or at room temperature.

Stuffed Baby Eggplants
Bharvan Chote Baingan

This makes a great meal when served with hot paratha or chapati. The soft flesh of the eggplants and the nutty filling give this special dish contrasting textures; the assorted ingredients add variety in flavor and taste. The filling (Steps 3, 4, and 5) can be prepared in advance.

INGREDIENTS
2 tablespoons fresh coconut, grated (See Chapter 7, page 160)
2 tablespoons peanut powder (See Chapter 7, page 165)
1 teaspoon sesame seed powder (See Chapter 7, page 161)
8 to 10 same-size baby eggplants (1 1/2 to 2 pounds)
6 tablespoons oil, divided
1 small onion, finely chopped
1 tablespoon ginger, finely chopped
1 tablespoon garlic, finely chopped
1 teaspoon cumin powder
1 teaspoon coriander powder
1/2 teaspoon red chili powder
4 tablespoons water
1 teaspoon salt
2 tablespoons lemon juice or tamarind water (See Chapter 7, page 167)
2 tablespoons fresh cilantro, chopped

METHOD
1. Have grated coconut and the peanut and sesame powders ready according to direction.
2. Wash and dry the eggplants.
3. In an appropriate size nonstick frying pan, heat 3 tablespoons oil on medium-high heat. When oil is hot (a piece of onion should sizzle as soon as it's dropped into the oil), sauté onions, ginger, and garlic until onions are soft.
4. Reduce heat to medium. Stir in cumin, coriander, and red chili powders into the onion mixture. Gradually add the 4 tablespoons of water while cooking the mixture, stirring constantly. When all the water has been added, the mixture will form a thick mass and oil will appear at the edges of the mixture.
5. Add salt, coconut, peanut and sesame powders, and lemon juice or tamarind water and continue to cook on low heat. When mixture thickens again, remove pan from the heat. Mix in cilantro. Let the mixture cool to room temperature.

6. To prepare eggplants for stuffing, two cuts are made across each individual eggplant to make a + sign. Start as if you are cutting the eggplant in half, lengthwise, but stop cutting just before you reach the crown. Then rotate the eggplant a quarter turn and make a similar cut, again stopping just before the crown. This will divide the eggplant into four quarters attached at the crown.

7. Divide the mixture into equal portions. Open each eggplant at the top. Fill the mixture between each section.

8. When all the eggplants are stuffed and ready to cook, heat remaining oil in the same pan on medium-high heat. Place eggplants in the pan. Reduce heat to medium. Cover pan while cooking.

9. Turn eggplants intermittently to brown them evenly and prevent burning. Test a few eggplants with a toothpick for tenderness. When desired tenderness is achieved, remove pan from the stove.

10. Serve eggplants hot or at room temperature.

CHAPTER 5
COOKING with CURRY PASTE
Peesa Masala

Our extended leisurely lunch is over, but the aroma of the mutton curry—cooked with roasted onions and whole spices—lingers. The pots are empty, and the food is drying on our fingers as the servants wait to clear the table. But on the veranda, we are still discussing and critically analyzing the curry and what made today's different from last time. Was it because of the additional ingredients, or was it the perfect roasting of mutton with *masala*? Maybe it was just the right heat to simmer the curry. Many questions with many answers, but no end to our discussion. The delectable taste of the curries remains fresh in my mouth, the memories fresh in my mind.

Growing up, I looked forward to Sunday—the day we could spare the time to discuss and learn more about cooking during our unhurried lunches. Each dish we prepared had a distinctive twist and needed plenty of time to prepare. My mother took a special interest in teaching and explaining each step. A strict vegetarian, she still made sure that we learned to cook both vegetarian and nonvegetarian dishes. She lovingly taught us how to make curries using onions and garlic, although she never included them in her own diet because she did not care for their smell and taste. She showed us how we could create an entirely new dish simply by making variations in the recipe.

Cooking with *masala* (curry paste) is a way of mixing spices unique to Indian cooking. Meat and vegetables are simmered with the *masala* to create a dish popularly known as curry in many countries. Curries are the main component of an Indian meal and are well known in the world of ethnic cuisine.

Masala is a Hindi word for spices. It also refers to ground fresh ingredients used in preparing various sauces for the curries. It is a generic term for spices, spice mixtures, or fresh ingredients cooked with spices. *Masala* may refer to just one spice or a combination of spices. For example garam masala is a blend of several spices. Onion *masala* is a ground mixture of onion, ginger, and garlic used in meat and vegetable curries.

The *masala* is the base for the curry. Fresh ingredients and spices are combined and cooked in oil. The vegetables or meat are then simmered in the *masala*. During the slow-cooking process, the meat or vegetables have a chance to release their juices into the *masala* and absorb the flavors from the spices. The final product is a dish with succulent, aromatic pieces of meat or vegetables with just the right amount of gravy.

Gravy is the thick liquid part of a curry created during the slow cooking of the dish. Gravy is also known as *shorba* or *rasa*. The thickness of the gravy depends on the ingredients used in preparing the *masala*. Onion, ginger, garlic, poppy seeds, coriander seeds, and nuts are some of the main ingredients used for the base in the curry. Onion paste—the combination of onion, ginger, and garlic ground together—is usually the first step in preparing *masala*. When roasted, the onion paste gives a distinct, sweet, caramelized fragrance to the curry and helps achieve the desired thickness for the gravy.

The flavor of a curry depends mainly on the way the spices are blended in the preparation. Blending the spices is an art you develop over time and with experience. It is at this step in the curry preparation that a cook can be creative. Here you have the opportunity to personalize an individual curry according to your preferred tastes.

You may decide to purée the onion, ginger, and garlic into a fine onion paste if you want a smooth-gravy curry. For a coarse and chunky gravy, however, start with coarsely chopped onion, ginger, and garlic. Use puréed tomatoes for the smoother gravy and coarsely chopped tomatoes for a coarse texture. For a creamy taste and a smooth gravy, you may also use yogurt or cream.

At this time, you also decide the spices. You may choose whole or powdered spices and add them at the various stages of preparation and cooking. You might decide to add the powdered spices to the onion paste prior to roasting or opt to add the spices after the onion paste is roasted in the oil or ghee. Another cook might use whole spices and add them to hot oil before roasting the onion paste so that they can slowly release their flavor, making the curry less hot. A clear idea of the final product's taste and appearance will help you select the spices and other ingredients that suit you best.

OBSERVATIONS and Helpful Tips

- The blender and food processor cut down on preparation time.

- Prepare onion paste beforehand and refrigerate or freeze.

- Nonstick pans allow you to use less oil and promote uniform cooking without burning ingredients.

- Keep pans covered when cooking onion paste to avoid splattering.

- Adjust the heat and stir the mixture frequently while roasting to avoid burning and scorching the *masala*.

Most Indian grocery stores carry several ready-made *masalas*. These *masalas* are a convenient option in our busy lives, but you will compromise some taste, flavor, and freshness.

The following spices, fresh ingredients, and dairy products are used to prepare the curry dishes in this chapter.

Spices	Fresh Ingredients	Dairy Products
Chili powder	Cilantro	Cream
Coriander powder	Green chilies	Sour cream
Cumin powder	Garlic	Yogurt
Cumin seeds	Ginger	
Garam masala	Onion	
Turmeric powder	Tomato	

In northern India, spices are generally used in powdered form; in southern India, whole spices are ground with liquid such as coconut milk, lemon juice, or tamarind juice. For certain types of curries, it's best to make the *masala* fresh the day you plan to cook the curry. These steps certainly help in determining the taste, texture, and aroma of individual curries.

In addition to basic spices such as turmeric, chili powder, and coriander powder, many other spices can be used. The spices you select will depend on whether the main ingredient is vegetable or meat. Spices such as fennel seeds, fenugreek seeds, and *ajwayan* are used with certain vegetables to give them a distinctive flavor. For meat curries, strong-flavored spices are often used. Spices like cinnamon, cloves, pepper, cardamom, or garam masala and other spice mixes offset the tough texture of meat. Meat takes more time to absorb the various flavors than vegetables.

In this chapter, I also introduce a new spice mix prepared by combining several whole spices (black peppercorn, cloves, cinnamon, black cardamom) in certain proportions. This combination of spices is known as garam masala, which literally means "hot spice." In India, each family prepares this mix using their own special recipe. You can easily prepare garam masala at home. (See recipe, Chapter 7, page 163.) You may also find garam masala at many Indian stores.

Preparing basic *masala*

To save time and maintain the freshness of *masala*, make the onion paste and roast it ahead of time. Roasted onion paste can be refrigerated up to one week and longer if it is stored in the freezer. Add selected spices for a specific curry to the roasted onion paste just before you start making the curry. This gives you the freedom to customize each.

The first step in making *masala* is to prepare the onion paste. To make the paste, peel onion, ginger, and garlic and coarsely chop them. For a smooth gravy, grind onion, ginger, and garlic into a paste using a blender. For a chunky and coarse gravy, chop the ingredients in a food processor. Add spices to the raw onion paste or add them after the onion paste has been roasted.

Roasting the onion paste. To make a smooth gravy, heat the oil on medium heat in a nonstick or heavy-bottomed pan. When the oil is hot, add ground onion paste and cover the pan to avoid splattering. Cook on medium heat, stirring occasionally, until most of the water has evaporated. At this stage, the mixture will change color from yellow-white to a light green because of the oxidation of onions. Uncover the pan and continue to cook the onion paste until oil starts to surface at the edges of the mixture.

For a coarse gravy, add chopped onion, ginger, and garlic to the hot oil in a nonstick or heavy-bottomed pan. Cook the mixture on medium heat, stirring frequently, until the onion mixture becomes soft and translucent. Reduce heat to low and continue to cook, stirring constantly until the mixture turns light brown and the smell of raw onions changes to a sweet, roasted smell. The oil will separate from the mixture, indicating it's time for the next step.

Add spices to the onion mixture and cook a little longer. To avoid burning, add water gradually while stirring constantly. During this step, the spices have a chance to release their flavors into the onion paste. Tomatoes, yogurt, or sour cream can be added later. Cook the mixture a little longer, until oil separates and produces a thick uniform mixture of *masala*. Individual recipes will give detailed information about when to add spices, tomatoes, yogurt, and the main ingredients for preparing the curry.

RECIPES

Potatoes and Peas Curry

Aalu Matar ki Subji

This recipe is a simple preparation with curry paste. The sweetness of peas adds a distinct taste to this dish. In India, peas are a winter vegetable—and well worth the wait.

INGREDIENTS

1 medium onion, chopped
1/2 teaspoon ginger, minced
1/2 teaspoon garlic, minced
1/4 teaspoon red chili powder
1/4 teaspoon paprika
1/4 teaspoon turmeric powder
1 teaspoon coriander powder
2 large potatoes (about 1 pound)
4 tablespoons cooking oil
1 large tomato, chopped
1 teaspoon salt or to taste
1 cup thawed peas
2 cups water
2 tablespoons fresh cilantro, chopped

METHOD

1. Purée onions, ginger, and garlic in a blender. Add chili, paprika, turmeric, and coriander. Let mixture sit for 10 minutes.
2. Peel and cut potatoes into 1-inch cubes.
3. Heat oil in a heavy medium-size saucepan. When oil is hot, add onion mixture and reduce heat to medium. Cook the mixture, stirring frequently to avoid burning or scorching, until it is golden brown and oil separates from the mixture.
4. Add tomatoes and sprinkle a little of the salt. Cover the pan. Cook, stirring mixture frequently, until mixture forms a smooth paste and oil separates from the mixture.
5. Add peas, potatoes, and remaining salt. Stir well to coat the vegetables with curry paste. Cover pan and cook on low heat for 5 to 10 minutes, stirring occasionally to avoid burning.
6. Add the water and simmer potatoes and peas on medium heat until potatoes are cooked.
7. Garnish with cilantro and serve the curry hot.

Red Kidney Beans
Rajma

Rajma, *a popular dish from the state of Punjab, is often served with boiled rice. Ghee gives a distinct taste to the beans. Adding garam masala during the last 5 minutes of cooking can bring additional flavor to the beans.*

INGREDIENTS

1 cup red kidney beans	4 tablespoons cooking oil
5 cups water	1/4 teaspoon red chili powder
1 1/4 teaspoons salt, divided	1 large tomato, chopped
1/4 teaspoon baking soda	1/2 cup yogurt
2 green chilies, cut lengthwise	2 teaspoons sugar
1 large onion, coarsely chopped	1 tablespoon ghee
2 teaspoons garlic, chopped	2 tablespoons fresh cilantro, chopped
2 teaspoons ginger, chopped	

METHOD

1. Soak beans overnight. Rinse beans before cooking. Place beans in a heavy saucepan with the water. Add 1 teaspoon of the salt, baking soda, green chilies, and 1 teaspoon each of the ginger and the garlic. Bring beans to a boil. Reduce heat to medium, cook until beans are soft and easy to mash. This step can also be done in a pressure cooker or slow cooker. (See Chapter 7, page 157.)
2. Place onions and remaining garlic and ginger in a blender. Add a small amount of water and run blender intermittently until the mixture makes a smooth paste.
3. In a medium saucepan, heat oil on medium-high heat. When oil is hot, add the onion mixture and cover pan to avoid splattering.
4. Reduce heat to medium. Stir onion mixture continuously and cook until most of the moisture is evaporated. Onion paste will change its color to green.
5. Stir in chili powder, tomatoes, and remaining 1/4 teaspoon salt. Cover the pan, stirring occasionally until tomatoes are cooked and turned to a thick mass.
6. Gradually add yogurt to the *masala* and cook for another 5 to 10 minutes until *masala* becomes thick and smooth.
7. Add cooked beans, sugar, ghee, and 1 tablespoon of the cilantro. Simmer for another 15 minutes on medium-to-low heat.
8. Garnish with remaining cilantro and serve hot.

Curried Garbanzo Beans
Chole

Chole is well-known and a popular dish from northern India. Many roadside vendors provide chole and bhatura as a snack. Chole is often served with bhatura or puri (deep-fried bread) to make a complete meal.

This dish tastes better if prepared ahead. Extra time allows the beans to become more flavorful. Another version is prepared with tamarind sauce.

INGREDIENTS
2 cups dried garbanzo beans
4 or more tablespoons + 6 cups water
2 teaspoons salt, divided
1/4 teaspoon baking soda
1 green chili, chopped
2 teaspoons ginger, chopped, divided
1 large onion, coarsely chopped
1 teaspoon garlic, chopped
4 tablespoons cooking oil
1/4 teaspoon red chili powder
1 teaspoon coriander powder
2 large tomato, chopped, or 1 cup crushed canned tomatoes
1 teaspoon garam masala (See Chapter 7, page 163)
2 tablespoons fresh cilantro, chopped

METHOD
1. Soak beans overnight in the 6 cups of water. Rinse beans before cooking. Cook beans in a heavy medium-size saucepan.
2. Add 1 teaspoon of salt and baking soda to the beans; bring to a boil. When white froth begins to form on the surface, remove it. Continue to boil until almost all froth formation stops.
3. Add green chili and 1 teaspoon of the ginger. Continue to cook on medium heat until beans are well cooked and slightly opened; they should crush easily with slight pressure. Cooking can also be done in a slow cooker or pressure cooker. (See Chapter 7, page 156.)
4. In a blender, place onions, garlic, and remaining teaspoon of ginger. Add a small amount of water and run blender intermittently until the mixture becomes a smooth paste.

SIX SPICES: A Simple Concept of Indian Cooking

5. Meanwhile, in a nonstick pan, heat oil on medium heat. When oil is hot, add the onion mixture and cover the pan to avoid splattering. Cook, stirring frequently, until onion mixture turns brown and most of the moisture is gone.
6. Stir in chili and coriander powders and a few tablespoons of water. Continue to cook. Add 2 to 3 more tablespoons of water so the mixture cooks well and the raw smell of onion and spices changes to a more roasted and aromatic smell.
7. Add tomatoes and remaining 1 teaspoon of salt, and cover the pan. Cook until mixture forms a smooth paste and the oil separates from the mixture.
8. Add *masala* to cooked garbanzo beans; mix well and bring to a boil. Reduce heat and let the beans simmer for another 15 to 20 minutes, stirring occasionally until desired consistency is achieved. Add garam masala in last 5 minutes of cooking.
9. Transfer garbanzo beans to a serving dish and garnish it with cilantro.

Mixed-Vegetables Curry

Rase wali Mili-Juli Subji

The combination of different vegetables makes this preparation a very nutritious dish. Each vegetable adds its unique texture and taste.

INGREDIENTS

6 cups assorted vegetables (carrots, cauliflower, turnips, potatoes, and peas)
1 large onion, coarsely chopped
1 teaspoon garlic, chopped
1 teaspoon ginger, chopped
1/4 teaspoon red chili powder
1/2 teaspoon turmeric powder

1 teaspoon coriander powder
7 tablespoons cooking oil, divided
6 tablespoons + 2 cups water
1 large tomato, chopped
1 teaspoon salt
1/2 teaspoon cumin seeds
2 tablespoons fresh cilantro, chopped

METHOD

1. Peel and cut all the vegetables into somewhat large but similar-size pieces.
2. Place onions, garlic, and ginger in a blender. Add a small amount of water and run blender intermittently until it makes a smooth paste.
3. Add chili, turmeric, and coriander powders. Run blender again to mix the spices into the paste.
4. In a medium saucepan, heat 4 tablespoons of the oil on medium-high heat. When oil is hot, add the onion mixture. Cover pan to avoid splattering.
5. Reduce heat to medium. Stir mixture continuously to avoid burning and scorching. Add 6 tablespoons of water, one tablespoon at a time, to prevent burning. Cook until most of the moisture evaporates. At this time the oil will separate from the onion paste, and the raw smell of onion and spices will change to a more roasted and flavorful smell.
6. Add tomatoes and a little of the salt. Cover the pan. Cook, stirring the mixture occasionally, until mixture forms a smooth paste and oil is separated from the mixture.
7. Heat remaining 3 tablespoons of oil in a large frying pan. When hot, add cumin seeds. Stir in all the vegetables and fry for 6 to 8 minutes.
8. Add fried vegetables and remaining salt to the *masala* (curry paste). Stir the mixture well so that all the vegetables are coated with *masala*. Cover and cook vegetables for 5 to 10 minutes, stirring occasionally to avoid burning.
9. Stir in 2 cups of water and let vegetables simmer on medium heat until potatoes and turnips are cooked.
10. Garnish curry with cilantro and serve hot.

SIX SPICES: A Simple Concept of Indian Cooking

Chicken Curry

Rase wali Murgi

When you use coarsely chopped fresh ingredients in the masala, *you add a grainy texture to the chicken curry.*

INGREDIENTS

2 to 3 pounds skinned chicken legs, thighs, and breasts

2 1/2 teaspoons salt, divided

6 tablespoons cooking oil, divided

1 large onion, finely chopped

3 teaspoons garlic, finely chopped

2 teaspoons fresh ginger, finely chopped

1 teaspoon cumin roasted and ground (See Chapter 7, page 161)

1 teaspoon turmeric powder

1 teaspoon coriander powder

1 teaspoon red chili powder

1/4 cup water, divided

1/2 pound fresh tomatoes, chopped

2 tablespoons fresh cilantro, chopped

6 tablespoons plain yogurt

1 teaspoon garam masala (See Chapter 7, page 163)

2 teaspoons fresh lemon juice

METHOD

1. Wash chicken pieces and dry with a paper towel. Sprinkle chicken with 1 1/2 teaspoons of salt and set aside.
2. In a heavy pan or nonstick frying pan, heat 2 tablespoons of the oil on high heat. When oil is hot, add chicken pieces a few at a time; fry for 3 to 4 minutes, or until they are white and firm, turning them once. Transfer chicken to a plate.
3. Add remaining 4 tablespoons of oil to the pan. Place onions, garlic, and ginger in hot oil. Cook on medium heat until onions are soft and golden brown.
4. Reduce heat to low. Stir in cumin, turmeric, coriander, red chili powder, and 2 tablespoons of the water. Cook for 1 to 2 minutes, stirring constantly. Stir in the tomatoes, 1 tablespoon of cilantro, yogurt, and remaining salt.
5. Increase heat to medium, add chicken pieces with the juices that have accumulated in the plate. Pour in remaining water. Bring to a boil, turning chicken over in the sauce to coat the pieces evenly.
6. Sprinkle curry with garam masala. Reduce heat to low. Cover and let curry simmer for about 20 minutes or until the chicken is tender.
7. Add lemon juice and remaining cilantro. Simmer another 5 minutes.
8. Serve hot with bread or over rice.

Fish Curry

Rase wali Machli

Fish is a main dietary component in most of the coastal regions of India. Preparation choices there include a variety of local ingredients such as coconut, tamarind paste, and mustard seeds.

INGREDIENTS

2 catfish fillets (about 1 pound)
1/2 teaspoon salt
3/4 teaspoon turmeric powder, divided
3/4 teaspoon red chili powder, divided
2 tablespoons fresh ginger, minced, divided
1 tablespoon lemon juice
1 medium onion, chopped
2 cloves garlic, chopped
1/2 teaspoon cumin powder

1/2 teaspoon coriander powder
6 tablespoons cooking oil, divided
1 cup water, divided
1 1/2 cups chopped tomatoes
1 teaspoon salt or to taste
1/2 teaspoon garam masala
   (See Chapter 7, page 163)
2 tablespoons fresh cilantro,
   chopped, divided

METHOD

1. Cut fish fillets into 2- to 3-inch pieces. Rinse fish under cold water.
2. Mix salt, 1/2 teaspoon of the turmeric, 1/2 teaspoon of the chili powder, 1 teaspoon of the ginger, and lemon juice in a bowl. Add fish, and marinate for 30 minutes.
3. Coarsely grind onions, remaining ginger, and garlic in a blender to make onion paste. Add remaining chili and turmeric, and cumin and coriander powders. Let mixture sit for 10 minutes.
4. Heat 2 tablespoons of the oil in a medium nonstick frying pan. When oil is hot, place fish pieces in a single layer. Fry them for 1 minute on each side. Remove them from the pan onto a serving platter.
5. Heat remaining 4 tablespoons of oil in the same pan. When oil is hot, add onion paste with the spices. Reduce heat to medium. Cook mixture and gradually add 1/4 cup of the water. Cook until golden brown and oil separates from the mixture.
6. Add tomatoes and salt. Cook until the paste becomes homogeneous and the oil separates from the paste.
7. Add remaining 3/4 cup of water to the roasted *masala* to make gravy. Bring to a boil on medium heat. Simmer for 10 minutes or until desired consistency is achieved.
8. Add fried fish pieces, gently coating them with gravy. Sprinkle with garam masala and 1 tablespoon of cilantro. Cover pan and let fish simmer in the gravy for 5 minutes. Uncover pan and gently turn the pieces for another 5 minutes or until cooked. Garnish the curry with remaining cilantro and serve hot with rice.

Curried Cheese Cubes and Peas
Matar Paneer Rase wala

This a rich-tasting curry usually prepared on special occasions. White cheese cubes (paneer) and green peas in a red tomato sauce give a festive look to this dish. This curry is quick and easy to prepare, provided you make the paneer *ahead of time.*

INGREDIENTS

1/2 cup onions, chopped	1 1/2 cups frozen or fresh peas
2 cloves garlic, chopped	1 teaspoon salt or to taste
1-inch piece of ginger, chopped	1/2 cup tomato sauce
1 3/4 cups water, divided	4 tablespoons nonfat sour cream
5 tablespoons cooking oil	1 1/2 teaspoons sugar
1/2 teaspoon turmeric powder	*paneer* (See Chapter 7, page 164)
1 teaspoon coriander powder	from 1/2 gallon milk, cut into 1/2-inch cubes
1/4 teaspoon red chili powder	4 tablespoons fresh cilantro, chopped

METHOD

1. Place onions, garlic, and ginger in a blender with 2 tablespoons of the water. Run blender on high speed to grind the contents into a smooth paste.
2. Heat oil in a heavy medium-size saucepan on medium-high heat. When oil is hot, add onion paste and cook, stirring often, until the paste turns golden brown. Add a spoonful of water occasionally to prevent burning and scorching.
3. Add turmeric, coriander, and red chili powders. Stir the mixture for few seconds. Cook further by adding water a little at a time until the mixture is well blended and makes a smooth *masala*.
4. Add peas and salt. Cook until peas are soft to the touch.
5. Stir in tomato sauce and turn heat down to low. Simmer for 10 minutes.
6. Add sour cream and sugar. Cook for another 5 minutes.
7. Add *paneer* cubes. Stir the mixture well to coat the pieces with *masala*. Add remaining water to the mixture. Simmer on low heat for 10 minutes.
8. Garnish with chopped cilantro and serve hot with rice or bread.

Shrimp Curry
Jhinga Rase wala

Shrimp curry is a delicacy in India. Shrimp dishes are prevalent in the coastal regions, where the catch is fresh and ingredients such as coconut are abundant.

INGREDIENTS

2 tablespoons lemon juice
1 teaspoon salt, divided
1 pound large shrimp (about 12 to 15), peeled and deveined
4 tablespoons cooking oil, divided
1 small onion, finely chopped
2 teaspoon ginger, finely chopped
2 teaspoons garlic, finely chopped
$^1/2$ teaspoon turmeric powder
$^1/2$ teaspoon red chili powder
1 teaspoon cumin powder
1$^1/2$ cups coconut milk
2 tablespoons fresh cilantro, chopped

METHOD

1. Mix lemon juice and $^1/2$ teaspoon salt in a bowl. Place shrimp in the bowl and marinate for 30 minutes.
2. Heat 2 tablespoons of the oil in a nonstick frying pan. Drain shrimp and reserve the marinade. Place shrimp in the hot oil; cover the pan and cook a few seconds, turning the shrimp and cooking until they are firm and have changed in color to pink.
3. Remove shrimp from the pan and set them aside.
4. Pour the remaining oil into the pan and heat on medium heat. Add onions, ginger, and garlic. Fry for 1 or 2 minutes, stirring continuously until onions are soft and translucent.
5. Add the turmeric, chili, and cumin powders to the onion mixture and stir. Pour the marinade into the pan and mix well with the onion paste.
6. Add shrimp and the remainder of the salt to the *masala*. Turn shrimp frequently to coat with the spices.
7. Pour the coconut milk over the shrimp and bring to a boil, stirring constantly.
8. Reduce heat to medium-low and simmer the curry for another 5 minutes. Add fresh cilantro into the curry and serve hot over boiled rice.

Lamb Curry with Cashews and Poppy Seeds
Mutton Kaju, Khus-Khus ke sath

This dish, with succulent pieces of lamb simmered in a creamy sauce, is an excellent choice to serve for any special occasion. Fragrant saffron, creamy cashews, and coarse poppy seeds add a mild taste and wonderful aroma.

INGREDIENTS

1/4 cup raw, unsalted cashew nuts
3 dried red chilies
1 tablespoon fresh ginger, chopped
3 garlic cloves, chopped
2 tablespoons white poppy seeds
1 teaspoon cumin seeds
3/4 cup water, divided
1/4 teaspoon saffron
1/2 cup cooking oil

1 medium onion, ground into a fine paste
1 1/2 teaspoons salt
6 tablespoons yogurt
1 1/2 pounds lean and boneless lamb, cut into 2-inch cubes
2 tablespoons fresh cilantro, chopped, divided
2 teaspoons fresh lemon juice

METHOD

1. Blend cashews, chilies, ginger, garlic, poppy seeds, and cumin seeds in a blender with 1/4 cup of the water at high speed for a few seconds to make a smooth paste.
2. Soak saffron in 2 tablespoons of the water.
3. Heat oil in a heavy saucepan on medium heat. When oil is hot, add ground onion paste and stir. Cover and cook for 5 to 6 minutes, stirring occasionally, until onion paste becomes light brown.
4. Stir in the ground spice paste. Cook the mixture on medium heat until oil separates from the mixture.
5. Add salt and yogurt. Cook for 4 to 5 minutes until most of the liquid has evaporated and the mixture forms a thick, dense mass.
6. Add lamb pieces and coat with spice mixture. Add saffron with its liquid. Cook for 2 minutes on low heat.
7. Stir and add remaining 1/2 cup of water. Cover pan and cook for 20 minutes.
8. Sprinkle 1 tablespoon of cilantro over the lamb. Stir occasionally until lamb is cooked.
9. Add lemon juice and garnish with remaining cilantro.
10. Serve hot with tandoori naan or chapati.

Egg Curry with Potatoes

Ande Aalu Rase wale

This egg and potato curry will please the nonvegetarian diner easily in the absence of a meat curry. It takes less time to prepare than meat dishes. Eggs, however, are still considered to be nonvegetarian by most Indians.

INGREDIENTS

1 large onion, chopped
1/2 teaspoon ginger, minced
1/2 teaspoon garlic, minced
1/4 teaspoon red chili powder
1/4 teaspoon turmeric powder
1 teaspoon coriander powder
2 large potatoes (about 1 pound)
4 tablespoons cooking oil

1 large tomato, chopped
1 teaspoon salt or to taste
2 cups water
6 eggs, hard-boiled and shelled
1/2 teaspoon garam masala
   (See Chapter 7, page 163)
2 tablespoons fresh cilantro, chopped

METHOD

1. Purée onions, ginger, and garlic in a blender. Add chili, turmeric, and coriander powders. Let mixture sit for 10 minutes.
2. Peel and cut potatoes into 1-inch cubes.
3. Heat oil in a heavy medium-size saucepan. When oil is hot, add onion mixture. Reduce heat to medium and cook, stirring frequently until onion mixture is golden brown.
4. Add tomatoes. Cook until the oil separates from the mixture, stirring occasionally to avoid burning and sticking.
5. Add potatoes and salt. Stir mixture so that all the potato pieces are coated with *masala*. Cover and cook on medium heat for 10 minutes, stirring occasionally to avoid burning or scorching. Adjust heat if necessary.
6. Add the water while stirring; bring curry to a boil. Add whole hard-boiled eggs. Simmer on low heat until potatoes are cooked and gravy has thickened to desired consistency.
7. Transfer curry to a serving dish, sprinkle with garam masala and garnish with cilantro.
8. Serve hot with fresh chapati.

SIX SPICES: A Simple Concept of Indian Cooking

Curried Meat Balls

Rase wale Kofte

Koftas are deep-fried ground meat and vegetable balls simmered with masala *to make* kofta *curry. This dish is considered a delicacy in the world of curry making. Koftas are very delicate, so you must take special care to prevent them from disintegrating in the gravy. Watch them closely while they simmer.*

INGREDIENTS FOR *KOFTA*

1 pound lean ground meat (chicken, lamb, turkey, or beef)
1 egg
2 to 3 tablespoons *besan* (chickpea flour)
1/2 teaspoon garlic salt
1/2 teaspoon garam masala (See Chapter 7, page 163)
16 whole blanched almonds or 4 dried apricots, each cut into four pieces

INGREDIENTS FOR GRAVY

1 medium onion, finely chopped
2 tablespoons ginger, finely chopped
2 large cloves of garlic, finely chopped
3/4 cup water, divided
5 tablespoons cooking oil
1 teaspoon cumin powder
1 teaspoon coriander powder
1/2 teaspoon red chili powder
1/2 teaspoon turmeric powder
1 cup tomato sauce
1 teaspoon salt
1/2 cup yogurt
2 tablespoons fresh cilantro, chopped

METHOD FOR PREPARING *KOFTA*

1. Heat oven to 400°F.
2. In a bowl, mix ground meat, egg, *besan*, garlic salt, and garam masala. Knead the mixture well or use a food processor for a few seconds until the mixture is smooth. Divide into 16 equal portions.
3. To make *kofta*, flatten the portions and place one almond or a piece of apricot on each one. Wrap the mixture around the nut or apricot to form a ball or *kofta*.

4. Place *koftas* on a greased baking dish. Bake for 20 minutes, shaking them occasionally to ensure even cooking all around. Remove the dish from the oven. Discard the fat, if any. Cover the *koftas* to keep moist.

METHOD FOR PREPARING GRAVY

1. Place onions, ginger, and garlic in a blender with 2 tablespoons of the water. Run blender on high speed to make a smooth onion paste.
2. To make gravy, heat oil in a heavy frying pan on medium-to-high heat. When oil is hot, add onion paste and cover the pan. When splattering stops, stir the onion paste and roast it until oil separates from the mixture.
3. Reduce heat to low. Stir in cumin, coriander, red chili, and turmeric powders to make *masala*.
4. Add a tablespoon of the water 3 to 4 times during the cooking. Cook the mixture for a few minutes, stirring constantly. The mixture will change into a thick mass.
5. Stir in the tomato sauce, salt, and yogurt. Simmer on low heat for 5 minutes.
6. Add remaining water to make the gravy. Increase heat to medium and bring to a boil.
7. Add *koftas* to the gravy and simmer on low heat for 10 to 15 minutes until desired consistency of gravy is achieved. Add more water if desired to make more gravy.
8. Serve the succulent meat balls hot with fresh naan.

Cabbage *Kofta* Curry

Patta-gobhi ke Kofte

Making kofta *curry is time-consuming. It involves several steps and many techniques to prepare, but the reward is worth the effort. The soft, succulent balls of cabbage are a wonderful transformation of, in my opinion, an otherwise unappealing vegetable.*

INGREDIENTS FOR *KOFTA*
1 small cabbage, shredded and steamed
1 cup *besan* (chickpea flour)
1/2 teaspoon garlic salt
1/2 teaspoon onion powder
1/4 teaspoon red chili powder
1/2 teaspoon coriander powder
1/2 teaspoon garam masala (See Chapter 7, page 163)
2 tablespoon fresh cilantro, chopped
1 tablespoon ginger, finely grated
cooking oil for frying

INGREDIENTS FOR GRAVY
1 medium onion, chopped
2 tablespoon ginger, chopped
2 large cloves of garlic, chopped
3/4 cup water, divided
5 tablespoons cooking oil
1 teaspoon cumin powder
1 teaspoon coriander powder
1/2 teaspoon red chili powder
1/2 teaspoon turmeric powder
1 cup tomato sauce
1 teaspoon salt
2 tablespoons sour cream
2 teaspoons sugar
1/2 teaspoon garam masala (See Chapter 7, page 163)

METHOD FOR PREPARING *KOFTA*

1. Let the steamed cabbage cool to room temperature. Squeeze most of the water out of the cabbage by squeezing between the palms of your hands.
2. Dry roast *besan* in a pan on medium heat, stirring constantly, until flour gives a roasted smell and changes color from yellow to light brown.
3. Place cabbage in a mixing bowl. Add garlic salt, and onion, red chili, and coriander powders. Also add garam masala, cilantro, and ginger. Gradually add roasted *besan*, mixing it with the cabbage and spices until it forms a soft, dough-like consistency. Set the mix aside for 10 to 15 minutes.
4. Divide mix into equal portions. Roll each portion into a 1-inch-diameter ball or *kofta*.
5. Heat oil, about 1 inch to 1 1/2 inches deep, in a wok or deep frying pan. Place a small portion of the mix into the oil to check if it's hot enough; it should surface immediately to indicate that the oil is ready.
6. When oil is hot, place a few *koftas* at a time in the oil and fry until they turn golden brown. Remove them from the oil and place on a plate lined with a paper towel.

METHOD FOR PREPARING GRAVY

1. Place onions, ginger, and garlic in a blender with 2 tablespoons of the water. Run blender on high speed to make a smooth onion paste.
2. Heat oil in a deep frying pan on medium heat.
3. Add the onion paste to the hot oil along with the cumin, coriander, red chili, and turmeric powders. Cover and cook the mixture on medium heat for 1 minute. Stir the mixture while cooking, adding water a tablespoon at a time.
4. Cook until oil separates from the mixture. Closely watch for any sign of burning.
5. Stir the tomato sauce into the curry paste to make the gravy.
6. Add salt; let gravy simmer for 5 minutes on low heat. Add sour cream, sugar, and the remaining water. Cook for another 5 minutes, stirring the gravy occasionally and mixing well.
7. Turn off the heat and set gravy aside until ready to serve.
8. Just before serving the curry, bring the gravy to a boil; reduce heat to low. Place *koftas* in the hot gravy and simmer for 10 minutes on very low heat, turning them occasionally so that the *koftas* can absorb the flavors from the gravy.
9. Place the *koftas* in a serving dish and sprinkle with the garam masala just before serving.
10. Serve *kofta* curry hot with Indian breads such as naan or puris.

Curried Stuffed Tomatoes

Bharvan Tamatar Rase wale

An eye-catching addition to the dinner table, this mouthwatering curry will please your guests' palates. The curry is a little sour in taste, but it makes the perfect main dish when accompanied by naan or chapati.

INGREDIENTS FOR FILLING

8 to 10 round, firm, ripe tomatoes (about 1 1/2-inches in diameter)
2 tablespoons cooking oil
1 small onion, chopped
1 tablespoon ginger, finely chopped
1/4 teaspoon red chili powder
1/4 teaspoon turmeric
1/2 teaspoon coriander powder
4 medium potatoes, boiled and mashed (1 1/2 to 2 pounds)
1/2 teaspoon salt
2 tablespoons cilantro, chopped

INGREDIENTS FOR GRAVY

1 medium onion, chopped
2 tablespoons ginger, chopped
2 large cloves of garlic, chopped
1/2 cup water, divided
tomato pulp (saved from filling)
5 tablespoons cooking oil
1 teaspoon cumin powder
1 teaspoon coriander powder
1/2 teaspoon red chili powder
1/2 teaspoon turmeric powder
1 teaspoon salt
1/4 cup whipping cream
1/2 cup plain yogurt
2 teaspoons sugar
1/2 teaspoon garam masala (See Chapter 7, page 163)

METHOD FOR PREPARING TOMATOES AND FILLING

1. Wash and dry tomatoes. To hollow out the insides of the tomatoes, use a sharp knife to cut around the stem end of each; carefully remove the stems, saving for later use. With a small spoon, carefully remove the pulp without breaking the skin. Save pulp for the gravy.
2. Heat oil in a nonstick frying pan on medium-high heat. Add onions and ginger, cooking for 1 or 2 minutes until onions become soft. Add red chili, turmeric, and coriander powders.
3. Add mashed potatoes, salt, and cilantro to the spice mixture. Cook potatoes, stirring them well into the spices, for 5 minutes.
4. Remove pan from the heat and let mixture cool to room temperature.
5. Divide the potato mixture into equal portions. Fill each tomato with the potato mixture. Replace the stem to cover the opening.

METHOD FOR PREPARING GRAVY

1. Place onions, ginger, and garlic in a blender with 2 tablespoons of water. Run blender on high speed to make a smooth onion paste. Use more water if needed. Transfer the onion paste to a bowl.
2. Place the saved tomato pulp in a blender and blend to make a smooth purée.
3. Heat oil in a deep frying pan on medium heat.
4. Add the onion paste to the hot oil along with the cumin, coriander, red chili, and turmeric powders. Cover and cook the mixture on medium heat for 1 minute. Stir the mixture and cook, adding water a tablespoon at a time.
5. Cook until oil separates from the mixture. Closely watch for any sign of burning.
6. Add puréed tomato and salt. Cook until mixture thickens and oil surfaces to ensure mixture's readiness.
7. Mix cream and yogurt in a bowl until smooth. Gradually add cream and yogurt mixture to *masala*, stirring constantly.
8. Add sugar. Reduce heat to low and simmer for 5 minutes. Add remaining water to make gravy; bring to a boil. Reduce heat to low.
9. Gently place all the tomatoes in the gravy. Cover the pan and simmer on low heat until tomatoes are soft to the touch and the skin has cracks. Sprinkle with garam masala. Cover the pan and remove it from the heat.
10. Keep the curry warm by keeping it in a moderately hot oven. Serve 1 tomato with a little of the gravy over a bed of freshly cooked rice to make an individual serving or serve stuffed tomatoes with chapatis.

BEYOND the BASICS
Recipes to Complete the Meal

In India each afternoon, street vendors set up

their roadside stalls, displaying mouthwatering savory snacks with hot and sweet-and-sour chutneys. Banging on the hot griddle, the hawkers try to attract the evening shoppers to the cart with their sizzling potato patties. People gather around and, one by one, they are soon served the spicy, hot, and enticing minitreats that help satisfy their hunger—without being too filling—until it is time for dinner.

Savory snacks are common throughout India. Indian cuisine is much more than just curries.

Crispy *samosa* and sweet tamarind chutney served with *chai*, the sweet Indian tea, are perfect afternoon snacks. No meal is complete without sweet, syrupy desserts flavored with saffron and cardamom. The tradition in India is to serve the sweets with meals, but sometimes they are offered as dessert at the end. Bread is a staple in northern India, and I can't even imagine an Indian meal without chapati or *paratha* or puri. Indian bread is usually prepared at home and served hot with meals.

I would be remiss if I neglected to mention the conclusion of an Indian meal. At both formal and informal gatherings, *paan, supari,* and a variety of *mukh-vas* are offered to guests to indicate the completion of the meal. These are traditional Indian mouth fresheners that also serve as digestive aids and postprandial stimulants. Culturally, by offering *paan* and *mukh-vas*, one can extend one's hospitality to the honored guest, seal a business deal, or simply share a friendship.

Paan is a heart-shaped betel leaf wrapped around soaked slices of betel nut (*supari*), lime, sweet rose preserve, tobacco, and a variety of seeds. *Mukh-vas* are dry mixtures of sliced or chopped betel nut mixed with an assortment of seeds (such as fennel and melon) or spices (such as cardamom, cloves, fragrant rose, saffron, and peppermint). *Paan* and *mukh-vas* are often available in prepared packages.

Artistically designed copper, brass, and silver containers serve as *paan-dans* or *paan* carriers. *Paan-dans* are specially designed ones with separate compartments for *supari*, lime, and other ingredients. The carefully crafted perforations allow air to circulate and keep the *paan* fresh. There are also specially designed containers with compartments to hold a variety of *mukh-vas*. The intricate patterns, delicate craftsmanship, and the uniqueness of these containers have made some of them collector's items.

To whet your appetite, I have included some additional delicious and popular recipes in this chapter. It includes my favorites for snacks, drinks, bread, and desserts.

The earlier recipes used only the six basic spices. These give you a better overall picture and understanding of Indian cuisine. You can add these new dishes to dinner menus with ease. By mixing and matching, you can create a new menu each day and truly appreciate the rich array of tastes and flavors that Indian cooking offers.

RECIPES

FRESH AND REFRESHING DRINKS

Tea
Chai

INGREDIENTS

3 cups water
5 teaspoons of sugar or to taste
2 pods of cardamom
1 cup 1% milk
2 teaspoons of loose tea leaves or 2 to 3 tea bags

METHOD

1. Place water and sugar in a saucepan and bring to a boil.
2. Crush the cardamom pods. Add them to the boiling water; let boil for 1 minute. Add milk and bring to a boil again.
3. Remove the pot from the heat. Add tea leaves or tea bags. Cover pan and let the tea steep for 2 to 3 minutes or until the tea leaves settle.
4. Strain tea into a teapot or remove the tea bags.
5. Serve hot.

Ginger Tea
Adrak Chai

INGREDIENTS
3 cups water
1 teaspoon fresh ginger, grated
1 cup 1% milk
5 teaspoons sugar or to taste
2 teaspoons loose tea leaves or 2 to 3 tea bags

METHOD
1. Bring water to a boil in a saucepan. Add ginger and let boil for about 30 seconds.
2. Add milk and sugar. When mixture comes to boil again, add tea leaves or tea bags.
3. Cover saucepan and remove from the stove. Let the tea steep for 1 or 2 minutes. Strain tea into a teapot or remove the tea bags.
4. Serve hot.

Mango Shake
Aam ka Rus

INGREDIENTS
1 cup mango pulp (peel ripe mango, scoop out pulp, and purée;
   or use canned mango pulp)
2 cups milk
6 tablespoons sugar
1 cup crushed ice
nutmeg powder

METHOD
1. Mix mango pulp, milk, and sugar in a blender. Run the blender to make a smooth pulp.
2. Add ice. Run the blender for 30 seconds.
3. Pour the mango shake into tall glasses. Sprinkle with nutmeg and serve.

Yogurt Drink

Lassi

This drink is best when blended just before serving.

INGREDIENTS

1 cup plain yogurt
1 cup water
1 cup milk
1/2 cup sugar

1 cup crushed ice
1/4 teaspoon cardamom powder
2 to 3 drops of rose water (optional)

METHOD

1. Place yogurt, water, milk, and sugar in a blender. Run the blender on high speed for 30 seconds.
2. Add ice and cardamom powder. Run the blender for 30 seconds.
3. Add rose water. Stir and serve in glasses with more crushed ice.

Mango Yogurt Drink

Aam ki Lassi

You should prepare this drink just before serving.

INGREDIENTS

1 cup plain yogurt
1 cup mango pulp (peel ripe mango, scoop out pulp, and purée; use canned mango pulp)

1 cup water
6 tablespoons sugar
1 cup crushed ice

METHOD

1. Place yogurt, mango pulp, water, and sugar in a blender; run it on high speed for 30 seconds.
2. Add ice and run the blender for another 30 seconds. Pour the drink into tall glasses with more crushed ice.

SIX SPICES: A Simple Concept of Indian Cooking

Litchi Yogurt Drink

Leechi ki Lassi

This drink is best when blended just before serving.

INGREDIENTS

1 cup plain yogurt
1 cup litchi nectar (available at Asian food stores)
1 cup 1% milk
1/2 cup sugar
1 cup crushed ice

METHOD

1. Place yogurt, litchi nectar, milk, and sugar in a blender; run it on high speed for 30 seconds.
2. Add ice and run blender again for another 30 seconds. Pour the drink in tall glasses and serve with more crushed ice.

Corn Fritters
Makki Pakoras

INGREDIENTS

1 15-ounce can of creamed corn
1 cup frozen corn kernels, thawed
1 cup *besan* (chickpea flour)
1 cup Cream of Wheat or semolina
1 small onion, chopped
1 or 2 green chilies, chopped
1/2 cup fresh cilantro, chopped
1 teaspoon salt or to taste
canola oil for frying

METHOD

1. Mix creamed corn, thawed corn, *besan*, and Cream of Wheat or semolina in a mixing bowl.
2. Add onions, green chilies, cilantro, and salt. Set the mixture aside for 10 minutes.
3. Heat oil, 1 inch to 1 1/2 inches deep, in a heavy, deep frying pan or wok on medium-high heat. When oil is hot, place teaspoonfuls of batter mix in oil until small portions of batter cover most of the oil.
4. Turn heat down to medium. Fry *pakoras* until they are golden brown.
5. Using a slotted metal spoon, transfer *pakoras* from the hot oil to a serving platter lined with a paper towel.
6. Serve hot or at room temperature with mint and cilantro chutney (see page 138).

Eggplant Fritters
Baingan Pakoras

INGREDIENTS

2 cups *besan* (chickpea flour)
1/2 teaspoon red chili powder
1/2 teaspoon cumin seeds
1 fresh green chili, chopped
3/4 teaspoon salt or to taste
water for batter (approximately 1/2 cup)*
1 medium-size eggplant
vegetable oil for deep frying

*Use of water varies from one batch of *besan* to another. For thicker batter, use less than 1/2 cup of water. For thinner batter, you may use a little more than 1/2 cup of water.

METHOD

1. Place *besan*, chili powder, cumin seeds, green chili, and salt in a bowl.
2. Add water gradually, to make a smooth batter. Let stand for about 15 minutes.
3. Wash and cut eggplant lengthwise into halves. Cut each half into 1/4-inch-thick slices.
4. Heat oil, 1 inch to 1 1/2 inches deep, in a heavy, deep frying pan or in a wok on medium-high heat.
5. When oil is hot, dip eggplant slices into the batter one at a time. Batter should flow smoothly over the eggplant slice, leaving a thin coating of batter over the eggplant.
6. Gently place each slice into the hot oil. Fry 6 to 8 *pakoras* at a time.
7. Fry on medium heat, turning frequently, until they are golden brown.
8. Using a slotted metal spoon, transfer eggplant *pakoras* from the hot oil to a serving platter lined with a paper towel.
9. Serve them hot, with mint and cilantro chutney (see page 138).

Mung Lentil Fritters
Moong Dal Pakoras

INGREDIENTS
1 cup yellow split lentils (*dhuli moong* dal)
$1/2$ cup water (reserved from the soaking water)
1 medium-size onion, chopped
$1 1/2$ teaspoons ginger, chopped
2 fresh green chili, chopped
$1/2$ cup cilantro, chopped
$1/2$ teaspoon red chili powder
$1/2$ teaspoon cumin seeds
4 tablespoons *besan* (chickpea flour)
1 teaspoon salt or to taste
vegetable oil for deep frying

METHOD
1. Wash yellow split lentils with 2 or 3 changes of water. Cover dal with water and soak for 4 to 5 hours.
2. Drain the water, saving $1/2$ cup. Place dal in blender, gradually adding $1/2$ cup of the reserved water, and grind into a smooth paste.
3. Place ground dal in a bowl. Add onions, ginger, green chili, and cilantro; mix. Add red chili powder, cumin seeds, *besan*, and salt. Mix well and set aside.
4. Heat oil, 1 inch to $1 1/2$ inches deep, in a heavy, deep frying pan or in a wok on medium-high heat.
5. When oil is hot, place teaspoonfuls of the dal mixture gently into the oil until most of the oil surface is covered. Fry 8 to 10 *pakoras* at a time.
6. Fry on medium heat, turning *pakoras* frequently until golden brown.
7. Using a slotted metal spoon, transfer *pakoras* from the hot oil to a serving platter lined with a paper towel.
8. Repeat the process until all the batter is used up.
9. Serve *pakoras* hot and crispy, with mint and cilantro chutney (see page 138).

Vegetable Fritters
Subji Pakoras

INGREDIENTS

2 cups *besan* (chickpea flour)
$1/2$ teaspoon red chili powder
$1/2$ teaspoon cumin seeds
1 fresh green chili
$3/4$ teaspoon salt
1 medium potato, peeled and thinly sliced
1 medium onion, peeled and thinly sliced lengthwise or assorted vegetables (see note)
water for batter (approximately $1/2$ cup)*
vegetable oil for deep frying
*Use of water varies from one batch of *besan* to another. For thicker batter, use less than $1/2$ cup of water. For thinner batter, you may use a little more than $1/2$ cup of water.

NOTE: Coarsely chopped spinach and cabbage, cauliflower florets, sliced zucchini, mixed chopped potatoes and onion slices, or any other desired vegetables will make great *pakoras*.

METHOD

1. Place *besan*, chili powder, cumin seeds, green chili, and salt in a bowl.
2. Add water gradually, to make a smooth batter. Set aside for about 15 minutes.
3. Heat oil, 1 inch to $1 1/2$ inches deep, in a heavy, deep frying pan or in a wok on medium-high heat. When oil is hot, dip each slice of potato into the batter and gently place it into the hot oil. Fry 6 to 8 *pakoras* at a time.
4. Fry on medium heat, turning frequently until they are golden brown.
5. After frying all potato *pakoras*, use a slotted metal spoon to transfer *pakoras* from the hot oil to a serving platter lined with a paper towel.
6. Mix the sliced onions into the remaining batter. Gently place 1-tablespoon portions of the mixture into the hot oil. Fry them in the same manner used for the potato *pakoras*.
7. Use a slotted metal spoon to transfer the onions from the hot oil to a serving platter lined with a paper towel.
8. Serve the vegetable fritters hot and crispy, with spicy mint and cilantro chutney (see page 138).

Potato-Stuffed Pastry
Samosa

INGREDIENTS FOR FILLING
4 tablespoons cooking oil
1 teaspoon cumin seeds
1 tablespoon fresh ginger, chopped
1 fresh green chili, chopped
1/2 teaspoon red chili powder
1 cup frozen peas, thawed
2 pounds potatoes, boiled and mashed
1 teaspoon salt
1 teaspoon dry mango powder
1 teaspoon garam masala (See Chapter 7, page 163)
1 teaspoon coriander seeds, dry roasted and powdered (See Chapter 7, page 161)
cooking oil for deep frying

INGREDIENTS FOR PASTRY
2 cups all-purpose flour
1/2 teaspoon salt
1/4 cup warm cooking oil
1/2 cup warm water

METHOD FOR MAKING FILLING
1. Heat oil in medium-size nonstick frying pan on medium heat.
2. When hot, add cumin seeds, stir for a second, add ginger and chopped chilies. Add chili powder and peas. Stir the mixture well.
3. Cook until peas become a little soft. Add potatoes, salt, mango powder, garam masala, and coriander; mix well
4. Heat the mixture on medium heat for 10 minutes, stirring occasionally. Let the mixture cool down before using. This mixture can be prepared ahead of time.

METHOD FOR MAKING PASTRY
1. Place flour and salt in a mixing bowl. Add warm oil gradually. Mix oil and flour with hands until mixture looks like bread crumbs.
2. Add water little by little, mixing into the flour gradually by hand, until it makes a soft dough. Cover and let stand for 15 minutes.

METHOD FOR ASSEMBLING *SAMOSA*

1. Divide dough into 12 equal portions. Roll each into a ball.
2. Flatten, one ball at a time. Roll out flat with the help of a little oil or dry flour. Make 5- to 6-inch disks, cut into two halves.
3. Lift one half at a time and moisten the edges with warm water.
4. Join the two ends of the straight side in such a manner that it forms a cone.
5. Press bottom of the cone together to close it.
6. Fill the cone with the potato filling leaving some room at the top to close it.
7. Close the cone by pressing the two sides of the pastry firmly.
8. Cover *samosa* with a damp cloth. Make all the *samosa* in the same manner.

METHOD FOR FRYING *SAMOSA*

1. Heat oil 2 inches deep in a heavy, deep frying pan or in a wok on medium-high heat. Oil is ready when a small piece of pastry placed into the hot oil surfaces immediately.
2. Place 5 to 6 *samosa* at a time into the oil. Fry them, turning occasionally until they are golden brown and the pastry becomes crispy.
3. Using a slotted metal spoon, transfer the *samosa* to a serving platter lined with a paper towel.
4. Serve *samosa* hot, with mint and cilantro chutney (see page 138) or the sweet-and-sour tamarind chutney (see page 137).

Cream of Wheat Porridge
Upma

INGREDIENTS

1 cup Cream of Wheat or semolina
4 tablespoons cooking oil
1/4 teaspoon black mustard seeds
1/4 cup raw peanuts or cashew nuts
2 dry red chilies
1 teaspoon *urad* dal
1 medium onion, coarsely chopped
10 to 12 fresh curry leaves
1/2 cup frozen peas
1 teaspoon salt or to taste
2 cups water
2 teaspoons sugar
1/2 lemon, squeezed for juice (about 2 tablespoons)
1/2 cup carrots, grated
2 tablespoons fresh cilantro, chopped

METHOD

1. In a heavy medium-size saucepan, dry roast Cream of Wheat or semolina on medium heat. Stir constantly for about 7 to 8 minutes until it is heated through.
2. Transfer to a dish.
3. Heat the oil in the same saucepan on medium heat. When oil is hot, add black mustard seeds. Cover the pan immediately. Keep covered until popping stops.
4. Add nuts and fry until golden brown.
5. Add dry chilies and *urad* dal; fry for 10 seconds. Add onions and curry leaves; cook until onions become soft.
6. Add peas and salt to onions; stir well. Add water. Bring the mixture to a boil on high heat.
7. Once the water is boiling, reduce heat to medium. Sprinkle the Cream of Wheat or semolina into the seasoned boiling water, stirring constantly to avoid lumps.
8. Reduce heat to low. Cook for another 5 minutes, until it becomes thick. Add sugar, lemon juice, and carrots; mix into the cooked porridge.
9. Remove pan from the heat. Transfer *upma* to a serving dish. Garnish with cilantro.
10. Serve hot or at room temperature.

SIX SPICES: A Simple Concept of Indian Cooking

Savory Pancakes
Oottuppum

INGREDIENTS
1 cup Cream of Wheat
1 cup rice flour
1 cup yogurt or buttermilk
1 3/4 cups water
2 tablespoons cilantro, chopped
1 green chili, chopped
1 teaspoon fresh ginger, chopped
1 small onion, chopped
1 teaspoon salt or to taste

METHOD
1. Place Cream of Wheat and rice flour in a mixing bowl. Mix yogurt or buttermilk and water separately until smooth.
2. Pour the yogurt mixture over the flour mixture, mixing them to make a smooth batter. Let it stand for 15 minutes.
3. When ready to make pancakes, add cilantro, chili, ginger, onions, and salt to the batter; mix.
4. Heat a nonstick frying pan on medium heat. Grease the pan with a few drops of oil.
5. Pour 1/4 cup of the batter onto heated pan; spread into a round shape with a spoon. Drizzle a few drops of oil over the pancake and cover the pan. Cook for few seconds, until it is browned like a pancake.
6. Turn the pancake over and cook for another minute uncovered.
7. Serve hot with coconut chutney (see page 139).

Crispy Tortilla with Potatoes and Garbanzo Beans

Chaat

This dish is a spicy mixture of boiled potatoes, garbanzo beans, and crispy tortillas dressed with yogurt sauce and sweet-and-sour tamarind sauce.

Chaat should be prepared just before serving. Often, potatoes, garbanzo beans, fried tortillas, yogurt, and tamarind sauce are placed on the table in individual dishes to be assembled individually by the guests, according to their liking.

INGREDIENTS

2 medium potatoes
1 teaspoon salt, divided
1 can garbanzo beans
4 flour tortillas, cut into small pieces
canola oil for frying
2 cups yogurt
1/2 teaspoon red chili powder
1/2 teaspoon roasted cumin seed powder (See Chapter 7, page 161)
tamarind chutney*
*Tamarind chutney is available in the Indian section of grocery stores or Indian food stores. You can also prepare it at home (see recipe, page 137).

METHOD

1. Boil, peel, and cut the potatoes into small cubes. Sprinkle 1/2 teaspoon salt onto potatoes. Place the potatoes in a serving dish. Drain the garbanzo beans; mix with the potatoes. Set the dish aside.
2. Heat oil, 1 inch to 1 1/2 inches deep, in a heavy, deep frying pan or in a wok. When oil is hot, add a handful of tortilla pieces; fry until golden brown. Remove them from the hot oil with a slotted metal spoon and place on a paper towel to drain excess oil and cool.
3. Mix yogurt with remaining 1/2 teaspoon salt until smooth; refrigerate. Just before serving, place tortilla chips over potatoes and garbanzo beans. Drizzle yogurt evenly over the mixture.
4. Sprinkle chili and cumin powders over the mixture. Drizzle with tamarind chutney.
5. Serve chaat immediately.

Potato Puff Rolls
Aalu Bhari Pastry

INGREDIENTS

4 medium potatoes, boiled and peeled
2 tablespoons cooking oil
1 teaspoon fresh ginger, chopped
1 to 2 green chilies, chopped
1 cup frozen peas, thawed
1/4 teaspoon red chili powder
1 teaspoon salt

3/4 teaspoon mango powder
1/2 teaspoon garam masala
  (See Chapter 7, page 163)
1/2 cup fresh cilantro, chopped
1 packet of puff pastry sheets
  (thawed and ready for use)
1/4 cup of milk

METHOD

1. Mash boiled potatoes into small pieces until they look like lumpy mashed potatoes.
2. Heat oil in a large frying pan on medium-high heat. When oil is hot, add ginger and green chilies and stir into the oil. Add potatoes and peas.
3. Reduce heat to medium. Add chili powder, salt, and mango powder to the potatoes and peas. Heat the mixture for 5 to 10 minutes until all the ingredients are mixed well and the mixture is heated through.
4. Remove pan from the heat. Mix the garam masala and cilantro into the mixture. Let the mixture cool.
5. Preheat oven to 350°F.
6. Unroll the pastry sheets. With the help of some flour, roll the pastry into a 14" x 9" rectangle. Cut the rectangle into 2 halves. (Two pastry sheets will make 4 halves.)
7. Divide the potato mixture into 4 portions.
8. Take 1 portion of the potato mixture and place it in the center of one half of the pastry sheet. Spread the potato mixture lengthwise to cover the full length of the pastry. Lift one edge of the pastry and turn it over the mixture. Brush a little milk over this turned pastry sheet. Lift the other edge of the pastry over so the edges overlap and you have a roll.
9. Lift the pastry roll and place it on a cookie sheet with seam side down. Brush the pastry with milk. Repeat the process until you've made 4 rolls. Place the rolls on two cookie sheets.
10. Place the cookie sheets in the oven and bake for 20 to 25 minutes or until the rolls are golden brown.
11. Remove the pastry rolls from the oven and let them cool for 10 minutes. Cut each roll into 1-inch pieces (about six pieces per roll). Serve warm with chutney or ketchup.

Potato Patty
Aaloo Tikki

INGREDIENTS
4 medium Idaho potatoes
1/2 cup bread crumbs
3 tablespoons cilantro, chopped
1/2 teaspoon red chili powder
1 teaspoon garam masala (See Chapter 7, page 163)
2 teaspoons mango powder
1 teaspoon salt
oil for cooking

METHOD
1. Boil, peel, and mash potatoes. Add bread crumbs, cilantro, chili powder, garam masala, mango powder, and salt.
2. Mix all the ingredients well in a mixing bowl. Knead to form a smooth ball.
3. Break off a handful of potato mixture. With the help of a little oil, roll it between your hands to form a flat and smooth patty. It could be round or oblong in shape.
4. Heat a greased heavy or nonstick frying pan over medium-high heat. When pan is hot, place a few patties at a time into the pan. Drizzle 2 to 3 teaspoons of oil around patties. Reduce heat to medium and brown the patties. Check for any signs of burning.
5. When they are golden brown, turn the patties over. Drizzle some more oil around patties and cook until other side is browned.
6. Serve patties hot with any chutney or tomato ketchup.

Tamarind Chutney

Imli Chutni

INGREDIENTS

1/4 cup dates, pitted and chopped
1/2 cup dry tamarind (See Chapter 7, page 167)
2 cups hot water
3/4 cup sugar
1/2 teaspoon salt
1/2 teaspoon red chili powder
2 teaspoons roasted and powdered cumin seeds (See Chapter 7, page 161)

METHOD

1. Soak chopped dates and dry tamarind separately, in 1 cup of hot water each, for 3 to 4 hours.
2. Use your hand to mix dates and tamarind in their soaking water to a make a pulp.
3. Put pulp through a strainer. Use extra water if needed to fully extract pulp.
4. Place pulp into a saucepan. Add sugar, salt, chili powder, and powdered cumin seeds.
5. Cook the mixture on medium-low heat, stirring occasionally. Bring chutney to a boil and cook for about 30 minutes on low heat until mixture thickens to the consistency of pancake syrup.
6. Remove pan from the heat and cover it. Once the chutney cools, store it in a glass container and keep refrigerated. Refrigerated tamarind chutney will keep fresh up to a month.
7. Bring tamarind chutney to room temperature before serving.

Mint and Cilantro Chutney
Pudina Dhania Chutni

INGREDIENTS
1 bunch of fresh cilantro
1 bunch of mint leaves
2 green chilies
1 lemon or to taste, squeezed for juice
1 teaspoon salt or to taste
1/2 teaspoon red chili powder
1/2 teaspoon cumin seeds

METHOD
1. Clean and discard brown leaves from the cilantro and mint. Wash the mint, cilantro, and chilies. Let them stand in a colander for a while to drain and remove excess water.
2. Coarsely chop the mint and cilantro. Place mint, cilantro, lemon juice, salt, chili powder, cumin seeds, and chilies in a blender. Blend on high speed until you achieve a smooth consistency.
3. Adjust lemon and salt according to taste.
4. Store chutney in a glass container and keep refrigerated. Refrigerated chutney will keep fresh up to a week.
5. Bring mint and cilantro chutney to room temperature before serving.

Coconut Chutney

Nariyal Chutni

INGREDIENTS

1/2 cup fresh coconut grated or fresh frozen coconut (See Chapter 7, page 160)
1 small onion, chopped
1 tablespoon fresh ginger, chopped
1 green chili, coarsely chopped
2 tablespoons lemon juice or to taste
1 teaspoon salt or to taste
1 tablespoon cooking oil
1/2 teaspoon mustard seeds

METHOD

1. Place coconut, onions, ginger, and chili in a blender. Blend intermittently for a few seconds. Add lemon juice and salt; blend until mixture forms a smooth purée. Transfer to a covered dish.
2. Heat oil in a small pan. When oil is hot, add mustard seeds. Cover the pan immediately and remove from the heat. When seeds stop popping, pour the seasoning over the coconut mixture; mix well. Adjust salt and lemon to taste.
3. Store it in an airtight container and keep refrigerated. Refrigerated chutney will keep fresh up to 3 days.
4. Serve coconut chutney at room temperature.

HOT AND SPICY BREADS
Deep-Fried Indian Bread
Puri

INGREDIENTS
2 tablespoons oil
2 cups whole wheat flour
1 to 1¼ cups lukewarm water
vegetable oil for frying

NOTE: You may roll and fry one puri at a time. Alternately, you can roll all the puris at the same time. Keep them moist by covering with a damp tea towel, then fry them one by one. Wrap puris in foil to keep warm.

METHOD
1. Mix oil and flour well in a bowl.
2. Add water gradually; mix it well by kneading frequently. Form into a firm dough. Knead the dough well, cover and set aside for 30 minutes.
3. Divide the dough into 18 to 20 equal portions. Roll each portion between your palms in a circular motion until smooth. Press the ball to flatten.
4. Grease rolling pin and board lightly with oil.
5. Use the rolling pin to roll each ball into a small, thin round disk (approximately 3 inches in diameter).
6. Heat oil, 1 to 1½ inches deep, in a heavy, deep frying pan or in a wok over medium-high heat. When oil is hot, place rolled puris one at a time into the oil.
7. Press lightly with a slotted metal spatula to help the puri puff up. Turn it over immediately and fry the other side.
8. Fry until both sides are golden brown. With the help of a slotted spatula, remove puris from the oil and place on a paper towel to drain oil.
9. Repeat steps 4 to 8 with each portion. Wrap puris in foil to keep warm.

SIX SPICES: A Simple Concept of Indian Cooking

Indian Flat Bread
Chapati or *Roti*

INGREDIENTS
2 cups whole wheat flour
1 to 1 1/4 cups of water
1 cup flour to roll chapati
butter or ghee

METHOD
1. Place flour in a mixing bowl. Add water gradually to make dough.
2. Knead dough, adding small amounts of water as needed, until dough becomes soft and pliable.
3. Cover and set aside for 15 minutes.
4. Divide dough into 10 to 12 portions. Roll each portion between your palms in a circular motion until smooth. Press to flatten.
5. Dust each flat ball with flour. Use a rolling pin to roll each flat ball into a circle, 5 to 6 inches in diameter. Dust with dry flour as needed to prevent sticking.
6. Place the chapati on a heated griddle or frying pan. Cook for a few seconds until light brown spots appear on the chapati. Turn chapati over to cook the other side. When brown spots appear on the second side, turn once more to the first side.
7. Press chapati with a folded kitchen towel to help it puff.
8. Remove chapati from the griddle and apply butter or ghee if needed.
9. Serve hot or store them in a covered, paper-lined container or wrap them in foil.

NOTE: On a gas stove, Step 7 can be done by directly placing the chapati on the open flame to let it puff. Turn the chapati over and cook for another few seconds.

Spicy Deep-Fried Indian Bread
Masala Puri

INGREDIENTS
2 cups whole wheat flour
$1/2$ teaspoon salt
$1/2$ teaspoon red chili powder
$1/2$ teaspoon turmeric powder
$3/4$ teaspoon *ajwayan*
2 tablespoons oil
1 to $1^{1}/4$ cups of warm water

NOTE: You may roll and fry one puri at a time. Alternately, you can roll all the puris at the same time. Keep them moist by covering with a damp tea towel, then fry them one by one. Wrap puris in foil to keep warm.

METHOD
1. Place flour, salt, chili and turmeric powders, *ajwayan,* and oil in a mixing bowl; mix well.
2. Add water gradually; mix it well by kneading frequently. Form into a firm dough. Knead the dough well, cover and set aside for 30 minutes.
3. Divide the dough into 18 to 20 equal portions. Roll each portion between your palms in a circular motion until smooth. Press the ball to flatten.
4. Grease rolling pin and board lightly with oil.
5. Use the rolling pin to roll each ball into a small, thin round disk (approximately 3 inches in diameter).
6. Heat oil, 1 to $1^{1}/2$ inches deep, in a heavy, deep frying pan or in a wok over medium-high heat. When oil is hot, place rolled *puris* one at a time into the oil.
7. Press lightly with a slotted metal spatula to help the puri puff up. Turn it over immediately and fry the other side.
8. Fry until both sides are golden brown. With the help of a slotted spatula, remove puris from the oil and place on a paper towel to drain oil.
9. Repeat steps 4 to 8 with each portion. Wrap puris in foil to keep warm.

Oven-Baked Roti with Fenugreek Leaves
Tandoori Roti Methi ke sath

INGREDIENTS
2 cups of whole wheat flour
$1/2$ teaspoon salt
$1/2$ teaspoon red chili powder
2 tablespoons dry fenugreek leaves (available in Indian grocery stores)
1 to $1^1/4$ cups of water
1 cup flour for rolling roti
butter or ghee

METHOD
1. Place flour, salt, chili powder, and fenugreek leaves in a mixing bowl.
2. Gradually add water to make dough. Knead dough, adding small amounts of water as needed, until dough becomes soft and pliable.
3. Cover and set aside for 15 minutes.
4. Divide dough into 8 to10 portions. Roll each portion between your palms in a circular motion until smooth. Press to flatten.
5. Dust each flat ball with flour. Use a rolling pin to roll each flat ball into a circle, 3 to 4 inches in diameter. Dust with dry flour as needed to prevent sticking.
6. Turn the broiler on.
7. Place 3 or 4 rotis on a lightly greased cookie sheet. Place the cookie sheet under the broiler.
8. Each roti will start to puff. A few brown spots will appear on the surface.
9. Remove the cookie sheet from the oven; turn each roti over. Place the cookie sheet under the broiler again. Cook until brown spots appear again on the roti.
10. Remove roti from the cookie sheet and apply butter or ghee.
11. Serve roti hot or store them in a covered, paper-lined container. Or wrap in foil to keep them moist and warm until ready to serve.

NOTE: In India, tandoori roti is normally cooked in a clay oven.

SWEET AND SENSATIONAL DESSERTS

Coconut Slice
Nariyal ki Burfi

INGREDIENTS

2 cups desiccated coconut
1 cup Carnation dry milk
3/4 cup sugar
1/2 pint whipping cream
4 tablespoons butter
4 pods cardamom, peeled and powdered
a few drops of yellow food coloring

METHOD

1. Mix coconut, dry milk, sugar, whipping cream, and butter in a large glass bowl. Microwave on high for 4 minutes. (Or you may place all ingredients in a heavy frying pan and cook on medium heat for about 20 minutes, stirring constantly until mixture thickens.)
2. Add cardamom powder and food coloring; mix well.
3. Microwave for 3 to 4 minutes, 1 minute at a time. At intervals, stir the mixture to keep from boiling over.
4. Once mixture forms a soft ball and does not stick to the bowl, transfer to a greased cookie sheet. Spread the mixture to 1/4-inch thickness.
5. Let stand for 30 minutes or until mixture cools.
6. Cut into 1-inch-square pieces. Store in an airtight container. Refrigerate after 2 days for longer storage.

Cream of Wheat *Halwa*
Sooji Halwa

INGREDIENTS

1 cup Cream of Wheat
1/2 to 3/4 cup ghee
8 to 9 almonds, chopped
1/4 cup raisins
3 cups warm water
1 cup sugar
1/2 teaspoon cardamom powder

METHOD

1. In a heavy saucepan, melt ghee. Add Cream of Wheat. Fry on medium heat until golden brown. Add almonds and raisins. Fry for another minute.
2. Carefully gradually add water to fried Cream of Wheat, stirring the mixture continuously to avoid lumps.
3. Increase the heat from medium to medium-high. Cook until mixture starts to thicken.
4. When mixture starts to thicken, add sugar. Reduce heat to medium-low. Add cardamom powder. Cook *halwa* until it stops sticking to the pan and pulls away from the edges.
5. Serve hot. This recipe can be prepared in advance and reheated just before serving.

Fried Noodles Pudding
Seviyan ki Kheer

INGREDIENTS

1/4 cup fine roasted noodles or *seviyan* (available at Indian grocery stores)
1 teaspoon ghee or unsalted butter
5 cups 2% milk
1/4 cup sugar
4 cardamom pods, peeled and crushed
1/4 teaspoon saffron
3 tablespoons sliced almonds, divided

METHOD

1. In a large, heavy-bottomed saucepan, melt butter or heat ghee on medium heat.
2. Break a handful of noodles and crush them.
3. Add noodles to the butter or ghee and fry them for 1 minute. Add milk. Simmer approximately 1 1/2 hours to get a thick, cream-like consistency.
4. Stir frequently to keep milk from sticking to the bottom of the pan.
5. When *kheer* is reduced to 3/4 of the original amount, add sugar, cardamom, saffron, and 2 tablespoons of the almonds. Cook another 10 to 15 minutes.
6. Remove from the heat. Cover and cool to room temperature.
7. *Kheer* can be served hot, cold, or at room temperature. Serve in individual dishes. Garnish with remaining almonds.

Fried Milk Balls in Syrup
Gulab-Jamun

INGREDIENTS
3 cups Carnation dry milk
6 tablespoons all-purpose flour
3 tablespoons Cream of Wheat or semolina
pinch of baking powder
1/2 pint whipping cream
3 cups sugar
3 1/4 cups water
6 cardamom pods, crushed
cooking oil for frying

METHOD
1. Place dry milk, flour, Cream of Wheat or semolina, and baking powder in a mixing bowl.
2. Gradually add cream to the mixture. Use 1/4 cup of water to make a soft dough and set it aside.
3. In a large, wide pan, add sugar and 3 cups water. Bring the sugar and water to boil to make a syrup. Add cardamom and simmer 5 minutes. Remove pan from the stove.
4. Meanwhile, gently knead the dough to make it smooth. Divide dough into 30 equal portions. Roll each portion of dough into a smooth ball.
5. Heat oil in a wok or frying pan on medium heat. The oil should be 3 inches deep in the pan for deep frying.
6. Place 8 to 10 balls into the heated oil and fry until they are golden brown. Stir the balls frequently in the oil to cook evenly.
7. Remove from the oil and place on a paper towel. Fry all the balls in the same manner.
8. Add fried balls to the warm (not hot) syrup. Let them soak for at least 3 to 4 hours. Gently turn them occasionally.
9. Serve at room temperature or warm them before serving.

Yogurt Cheese and Saffron Pudding
Shrikhand

INGREDIENTS
2 32-ounce plain yogurt cartons (makes 4 cups yogurt cheese)
1/4 teaspoon saffron threads
2 tablespoons warm water
1 cup sugar or according to taste
a few drops of yellow food coloring (optional)
1/4 teaspoon nutmeg
1 tablespoon almonds, chopped
1 tablespoon pistachios, chopped

METHOD
1. Make yogurt cheese: Line a colander with a damp cheesecloth. Place colander in a bowl to catch drained liquid. Pour yogurt from the container into the cloth. Cover and refrigerate yogurt for 8 to 10 hours, to drain completely. Save the solid contents (yogurt cheese) from the colander and discard the liquid. (You can substitute yogurt cheese with plain Greek yogurt to save time.)
2. Place saffron threads in the warm water; soak for 10 minutes.
3. Mix yogurt cheese and sugar in a mixing bowl with a hand mixer at low speed, until it forms a smooth texture.
4. Add saffron with its soaking water, yellow food coloring, and nutmeg. Stir for another minute to mix well.
5. Transfer contents to a serving bowl or individual serving dishes. Decorate pudding with chopped nuts. Chill the pudding before serving.

SIX SPICES: A Simple Concept of Indian Cooking

Rice Pudding
Chawal ki Kheer

INGREDIENTS
1/4 cup basmati rice
8 cups 2% milk
1/2 cup sugar
4 cardamom pods, peeled and crushed
1/4 teaspoon saffron
3 tablespoons sliced almonds, divided
2 tablespoons golden raisins

METHOD
1. Wash and soak rice for 15 minutes in a bowl.
2. In a large, heavy-bottomed saucepan, heat milk over medium heat and bring to a boil.
3. Add soaked rice to the milk. Let simmer for 1 1/2 hours, stirring frequently to keep from sticking to the bottom of the pan.
4. When *kheer* is reduced to 3/4 of the original amount, add sugar, cardamom, saffron, 2 tablespoons almonds, and raisins. Cook 10 to 15 minutes.
5. Remove from the heat. Cover and cool to room temperature.
6. *Kheer* can be served hot, cold, or at room temperature. Serve in individual dishes. Garnish with remaining almonds.

CHAPTER 7
TIPS and TECHNIQUES

Preparing Indian dishes and curries can be a fun

and exciting experience. It can also be intimidating and time-consuming without proper instructions. By planning in advance and using certain appliances, you will cut down on your time in the kitchen. Indian cooking will then become rewarding.

In this chapter, I have included some suggestions on how to get yourself and your kitchen ready before you start preparing a dish so that the cooking will go smoothly. I also provide essential information about some ingredients commonly found in Indian cuisine and directions for using and preparing them.

Read the recipes

Review a recipe carefully beforehand so you'll know all the ingredients required to prepare the dish. Make a grocery list of those you need to buy. Having the ingredients ready in advance makes for a smooth transition between each step in a recipe.

Choose the right utensils

The pot or pan you select is critical to the success of a dish. The appropriate size pot or pan results in proper and faster cooking. If you choose a pan that is too small for the amount of food you are cooking, it will be difficult to stir contents properly and the spices and vegetables will not mix well. If the pan is too large for the quantity of vegetables, the vegetables will burn very easily. Heavy-bottomed saucepans ensure uniform cooking and are recommended for dishes that call for a slow simmer. Using a nonstick frying pan reduces fat consumption. Make sure you have the correct size lids for the pans. Properly covered pans help retain the flavor of a dish and facilitate faster cooking.

In the recipe instructions, I use the terms small, medium, and large to indicate the pan size. For saucepans, small means a 1- to 2-quart pan; medium is a 2- to 4- quart pan; and large is a pan with a capacity of more than 4 quarts. For frying pans, a small pan means an 8-inch frying pan; medium is a 10- to 12-inch one.

Most of my recipes serve four to six people. If you want to double the recipe, you should use a large skillet instead of a large frying pan and a Dutch oven instead of a large saucepan to accommodate the larger amounts.

Prepare the ingredients

Before you begin cooking, you'll want to have all the main ingredients ready in the form the recipe requires. Cut, chop, or dice the vegetables and meat according to the directions. Assemble all the spices in the order you will be using them. Have other ingredients ready in the form (powdered, grated, or roasted) required for cooking.

The recipes may call for ingredients that need additional preparation time. Prepare these well in advance and store them for later use. For example, roasted cumin powder is not generally available in stores and therefore it needs to be made at home. Raw cumin seeds must be roasted in a pan and cooled before you can grind them into powder.

Know the unfamiliar ingredients

Some ingredients in my recipes—such as curry leaves, coconut, and tamarind—are not commonly used in western cooking. Some of them may be available in regular grocery stores in the fresh produce section, but others are only found in Indian stores or ethnic food stores. This chapter offers clear instructions so you will be able to prepare these ingredients at home.

To help you gain a better understanding and knowledge of unusual ingredients and how they are used in the Indian cooking, I will explain their characteristics. I will also tell you where to find the ingredients in a store, how to get them ready for use, and how to keep them for later use. I hope that the detailed explanations and proper preparation of these ingredients will enable you become more comfortable and confident while using them.

OBSERVATIONS and Helpful Tips

Modern technology can help you save time. Using the following kitchen appliances will make your cooking experience less tedious—thereby making the time you spend preparing Indian dishes more pleasurable.

- Use a blender to grind and purée fresh ingredients.
- Use a coffee grinder or blender to powder spices.
- Use a rice cooker to cook rice.
- Use a pressure cooker to cook lentils, beans, and meat curries.

The following ingredients
—and methods for preparing and storing them—
are explained in detail in this chapter.

Beans and lentils
Bean sprouts
Butternut squash
Coconut
Curry leaves
Dry roasting whole spices (cumin and coriander seeds)
Eggplant
Garam masala
Ghee
Paneer
Peanuts
Rice
Tamarind

Beans and Lentils

Beans and lentils are used extensively in everyday meals. They are an important source of protein in the predominantly vegetarian diet of India. In Indian cooking, beans and lentils fall into the general category of legumes, known as dal in India.

Beans are often used whole. Lentils can be whole, split with skin (*chilke wali* dal), or split without skin (*dhuli* dal). Lentils can also be soaked and ground into a paste to make dough for dishes like *dosa* (rice and *urad* dal pancakes), and *dahi-wada*. Different lentil flours are used to make sweets and snacks.

Facts about lentils and beans
- Beans and lentils are in the family of legumes.
- Soaking beans well before cooking or overnight cuts down on cooking time.
- Whole lentils take a shorter time to cook than beans. They do not require prior soaking.

SIX SPICES: A Simple Concept of Indian Cooking

- Cooking time varies from a few minutes to a few hours, depending on the variety of bean or lentil.
- Split lentils and lentils without skin take less time to cook than whole lentils.
- Lentils are cooked with salt and turmeric. Beans are cooked with salt, garlic, and ginger.
- Both beans and lentils may cause gastric discomfort.
- Spices such as asafetida and fresh ingredients such as ginger, garlic, and onion improve the digestibility of beans and lentils.
- Beans and lentils can be cooked in a saucepan, a slow cooker, or a pressure cooker.

PREPARING BEANS AND LENTILS FOR COOKING

1. Place dry beans or lentils on a tray to check for and remove any stones, husks, or discolored beans. Repeat the process until the quantity you need is cleaned.
2. Wash the beans or lentils with 3 to 4 changes of water or until the water runs clear.
3. Soak whole beans for 8 to 10 hours or overnight before cooking.
4. Whole lentils can be cooked without prior soaking, but soaking them for 1 to 2 hours will cut down on cooking time.
5. Pressure cooking is the preferred way to cook beans and lentils in India because the cooking time is much shorter than using a saucepan or slow cooker.
6. Use a saucepan or slow cooker if time is not a factor.

COOKING BEANS AND LENTILS IN A SAUCEPAN

1. Use medium-size saucepan for 1 cup of beans or lentils.
2. Place washed beans or lentils in the pan with required amount of water (see chart, page 158). Add salt and turmeric or other ingredients according to the recipe.
3. Bring to a boil on high heat; reduce heat and simmer. Skim off any froth that develops and discard.
4. Cover the pan, leaving a small gap to keep from boiling over. Watch carefully for any boiling over.
5. Cook beans and lentils until they become thick and soup-like in consistency (see chart, page 158).
6. You may need to add more water or increase the recommended cooking time (see chart, page 158). The time depends on the evaporation of water during cooking.

COOKING BEANS AND LENTILS IN A SLOW COOKER

1. Using a slow cooker is the easiest and most worry-free way of cooking beans and lentils.
2. Place washed beans or lentils in the slow cooker with the required amount of water (see chart, page 158). Add salt, and turmeric or ginger, and garlic according to recipe.

Cooking Times and Water Amount for Beans and Lentils

- Red kidney beans (*rajma*) and garbanzo beans or chickpeas (*chole*)

Saucepan	5 cups water	cook for 3–4 hours
Pressure cooker	4 cups water	cook for 20 minutes
Slow cooker	4 cups water	cook for 6–8 hours

- Pigeon peas (*toor* dal or *arhar* dal)

Saucepan	5 cups water	cook for 40 minutes
Pressure cooker	4 cups water	cook for 5 minutes
Slow cooker	4 cups water	cook for 3–4 hours

- Black-eyed peas (*rongi* or *lobia*) and brown lentils (*masoor* dal)

Saucepan	5 cups water	cook for 2 hours
Pressure cooker	4 cups water	cook for 20 minutes
Slow cooker	4 cups water	cook for 6 hours

- Whole mung beans (sabat *moong* or *mug*)

Saucepan	5 cups water	cook for 2 hours
Pressure cooker	4 cups water	cook for 20 minutes
Slow cooker	4 cups water	cook for 6 hours

- Washed mung beans (*dhuli moong* dal) and red lentils (*lal* dal)

Saucepan	5 cups water	cook for 20–25 minutes
Pressure cooker	*Pressure cooking not recommended*	
Slow cooker	4 cups water	cook until beans are soft

3. Cook on high heat for 2 hours, then reduce to cook slowly.
4. Cook beans and lentils to desired consistency. Allow 6 to 8 hours for beans and 3 to 4 hours for lentils.

COOKING BEANS AND LENTILS IN A PRESSURE COOKER

1. Read instruction manual carefully and follow all safety rules for pressure cooking. This method can be dangerous if safety rules are ignored.
2. Place washed beans or lentils in the pressure cooker with the required amount of water (see chart, page 159). Add salt, and turmeric or ginger, and garlic according to recipe.

3. Bring to a boil on medium-high heat. Skim off any froth that develops and discard.
4. Close pressure cooker and place pressure weight in place. Once pressure develops, reduce heat to medium and cook under pressure for desired time (see chart, page 158).
5. Remove pressure cooker from the stove. Let the pressure drop by itself, which takes some time.
6. To drop pressure more quickly, cool the pressure cooker under cold running water.
7. Remove the pressure weight and open the lid. Never force open the lid on a pressure cooker.

The chart on page 158, gives approximate amounts of water and cooking times for some of the beans and lentils after they have been washed and soaked. Heat intensity and water evaporation during the cooking are two factors that affect actual cooking time. After a while you will learn to cook perfect beans and lentils, judging them by their taste, the time required to cook them, and the right amount of water it takes.

Bean Sprouts

The two most common sprouted beans used in Indian cooking are whole *moong* and *kala chana* (black gram), but any kind of whole bean or seed will sprout. Bean sprouts are nutritious and tasty ingredients in our daily meals. Using a few simple steps, you can sprout beans at home and add this healthy alternative to your diet. I have used *moong* beans to explain the process. They are green, shiny, and oblong in shape. You can find them at most grocery stores. In Indian cooking, sprouts are kept short, up to 1/2 inch long.

To sprout *moong* beans, take 1 cup of beans. Clean and discard any discolored ones. Wash in cold water several times until water is clear. Soak them in warm water for 8 to 10 hours or overnight. After soaking, beans swell and increase in size. Discard all the soaking water and rinse the beans with fresh cold water. Place in a colander lined with a paper towel or a clean tea towel. (Beware that beans may leave a permanent stain on your towel.) Cover with a paper towel and then with a plate. Keep the colander on a plate and place in a warm place for 24 hours. Keep the beans moist by sprinkling them with water after 10 to 12 hours.

After 24 hours, we can see about 1/2-inch-long sprouts on the beans. For longer sprouts, let them grow for another day or until desired length is achieved. Sprouting takes less time in summer than it does in winter.

Transfer the sprouts to an air-tight container and refrigerate them for future use. The sprouts will remain fresh up to one week. One cup of *moong* beans makes approximately 3 to 4 cups of sprouted beans. Sprouts can be used raw or cooked, in salads, sandwiches, or as a side dish.

Butternut Squash

To cook and purée butternut squash, cut into big pieces. Place in a shallow dish with 1 cup of water. Cover and microwave on high until squash becomes soft and tender. You can also steam squash pieces in a steamer or pressure cooker. When the squash is cool enough to handle, remove the skin. Mash the squash with a fork until smooth. The mashed pulp can be refrigerated for 2 to 3 days or it can be kept in the freezer 1 to 2 months for future use.

Coconut

Coconut is a tropical fruit, available year-round in coastal areas around India and on many tropical islands. In the United States, fresh coconut can be found in many supermarkets all year. In India, coconut has religious significance. It is also one of the main ingredients in southern India. Fresh coconut and coconut milk are used for many curries and other dishes in this region.

Dry coconut. In northern India, dry coconut is commonly used because fresh coconut is not readily available. Dried coconut is usually grated and used as a complementary ingredient in sweets and desserts. Another form of coconut is fine, grated, dehydrated coconut, also used in sweets and other preparations. Desiccated coconut is used as a substitute for fresh coconut in some recipes. For convenience, consider using fresh-frozen grated coconut. You will find both desiccated and frozen coconut at Indian food stores.

Fresh coconut. When selecting fresh coconut, choose one without any mold or cracks. Some coconuts have center lines or cracks across the fruit for easy breaking. Shake the coconut to check if enough water is present to ensure freshness. Press the three eyes on top of the shell to check for firmness. A soft eye indicates the fruit may be rotten.

To break a fresh coconut, place it on a concrete surface. Hold the coconut firmly and tap with a hammer around the center of the shell until it cracks. Once the shell cracks, coconut water will come out. When all the water is drained, hit the coconut with the hammer to break the coconut into two halves. Carefully remove the white flesh with a knife. Sometimes heating the coconut halves in a microwave or regular oven for a few minutes can make this process easier.

Remove the dark skin from the white meat with a peeler or knife. Grate the coconut with a grater or shred in a food processor. Shredded coconut can be refrigerated for 1 or 2 days. For longer storage, freeze the shredded coconut in small portions for future use.

Coconut milk. Many recipes call for coconut milk. You can make coconut milk simply by grinding the shelled and peeled white coconut flesh with hot water in a blender. Place half of a coconut that has been cut into small pieces into a blender with 1/4 cup hot water. Run the blender for a few seconds to grind the coconut. Add an additional 1 cup of hot water and run the blender for a few more seconds until the coconut forms a smooth purée. Strain through a cheesecloth to separate the liquid from the grated flesh. Remove excess liquid by twisting and squeezing the cheesecloth around the coconut. This liquid is referred to as coconut milk. Repeat the process with additional hot water to fully extract the milk from the coconut. The remaining coconut can be saved and used in cooking or garnishing.

Desiccated coconut. This form of coconut is a finely grated, powdery, dehydrated coconut. It is available prepackaged at most of Indian food stores. When fresh coconut is not available, I use desiccated coconut that I soak in warm milk for 10 minutes. The coconut absorbs all the milk and becomes moist and soft. By using this process you'll have a good substitute for fresh coconut without compromising taste.

Curry Leaves

The curry plant is native to India, where it is found extensively except in the very cold northern region. Curry leaves are the fresh leaves of the plant. These dark green, aromatic leaves have a distinct taste and fragrance. You will find fresh curry leaves at many Indian grocery stores.

Curry leaves stay fresh for only a short time. They are very delicate but can be refrigerated for up to 1 week without losing their fragrance. For longer periods, store the leaves in the freezer. The leaves have no fragrance once they are dried, so do not waste your money buying these.

When purchasing fresh curry leaves, store a portion in the freezer and refrigerate the remaining leaves for immediate use. To refrigerate, wrap the unwashed leaves in a paper towel and place them in a plastic bag or a plastic container. Wash the leaves just before using. To freeze, place unwashed curry leaves in a plastic bag and place the bag in the freezer. Take the leaves out and rinse them before using as a seasoning.

In Indian cooking curry leaves are used to flavor various curry, yogurt, and salad dishes. When placed in hot oil, the leaves impart their delicate fragrance. The vegetables cooked in this fragrant hot oil give a very distinct taste and aroma to the dish.

Dry Roasting Whole Spices

Dry roasting whole spices is a simple process often used in Indian cooking to prepare various spice mixtures or individual powdered spices. Cumin seeds are one of the most commonly roasted spices. They are used in flavoring many yogurt dishes, salads, and some curries. Seeds like coriander, fennel, sesame, and cumin are some of the whole spices that are roasted and powdered to achieve a toasted aroma and taste. As they are heated, the whole spices release their scent and give a unique nutty flavor and zest to certain dishes. Raw powdered spice has a much milder taste and smell than the roasted powder.

Roasted spices have a long shelf life when stored properly. Roasting whole spices first also helps make grinding easier. When spices are heated, the moisture evaporates, leaving the spice grains dry and brittle. Easier grinding produces a more finely powdered spice.

You will not find roasted spices in stores, so you generally must prepare them at home. To save time when making a recipe, you should roast and powder these spices in advance.

To roast any whole spice, take the desired quantity of seeds. Place them on a heavy iron griddle or pan on medium-to-high heat. Stir the seeds with a spatula to avoid scorching and to evenly roast. After a few minutes, the seeds will release their scent and become more aromatic. Continue to roast seeds until desired color and smell is achieved. The seeds will be light brown and have a stronger smell. Some seeds may start to crackle during the roasting, indicating that roasting is complete. Small amounts of seeds can also be roasted in a microwave; roasting a large amount of seeds in the microwave will result in uneven roasting.

Remove the pan from the heat and transfer the seeds to a plate to cool. Place the roasted seeds in a coffee grinder or a blender and grind to the desired texture. (A mortar and pestle can also be used.) For a fine powder, sift the powdered seeds and repeat the process of grinding and sifting until the desired texture is achieved. Grinding small portions at a time makes the process easier.

Eggplant

You can prepare eggplant *raita* and eggplant *bhurta* quickly if you have roasted and ready-to-use eggplant pulp. Dishes made with roasted eggplant are especially delicious if the roasting is done over charcoal, which gives a special smoked flavor to the eggplant. For a simple and clean method, try broiling eggplant in your oven. Roasted eggplant pulp can be refrigerated for only a few days, but it freezes well and can be stored for a long time.

Try roasting eggplant in August and September, when the vegetable is plentiful and inexpensive. Select those that are plump, fleshy, and shiny. To roast under the broiler, wash the eggplant, remove the crown, and cut in half lengthwise. Place the flesh side down on a greased cookie sheet. Using the broiler setting, roast the eggplants for 20 to 30 minutes or until the inside flesh becomes soft. Remove from the oven and let the eggplant cool. Scoop out the flesh carefully and discard the skin.

A good time to roast eggplant over charcoal is after you have finished grilling meat and the coals have begun to cool. To roast eggplant on a grill, first wash the eggplant. Make a few deep cuts on the skin with a sharp knife. Place it whole on the grill. For even roasting, turn the eggplant frequently. The slower heat from the charcoal roasts the flesh deep inside. The outer skin burns, giving the eggplant its smoked flavor. When all sides are browned and the eggplant is soft to the touch, remove it and let it cool. Place the eggplant under cold running water to remove the burned skin. Using a knife, dice the roasted flesh to make a smooth pulp.

Garam Masala

The literal translation of "garam masala" is "hot spice." Garam masala is a powdered blend of spices. This mix of spices not only gives a sharp taste to a dish, but can also make it hot. Use garam masala selectively and with care.

You can prepare garam masala easily at home or purchase it as a ready-made mix. Several brands of garam masala are available in specialty stores and ethnic sections of grocery stores.

When making garam masala, you combine whole spices in certain proportions and grind them to make a powder. The recipe for this blend may vary from family to family and from cook to cook. The flavor of the mixture also varies with the selection of spices in the mix.

The main ingredients used in garam masala are black pepper, large brown cardamom pods, cloves, cinnamon, and nutmeg. Some cooks also use bay leaves, cumin seeds, and coriander seeds. The quantity of each ingredient in relation to the other ingredients determines the potency, flavor, and color of this spice mixture.

To prepare garam masala, lightly dry roast all ingredients individually. After cooling them, grind the spices separately in a coffee grinder to a powdery texture. Then mix and sift powdered spices to achieve a fine powder.

Here is my recipe for garam masala:

INGREDIENTS
4 brown cardamom pods
1 cinnamon stick
1 tablespoon black cumin seeds
1 tablespoon whole black peppercorns
1 tablespoon whole cloves
1/2 teaspoon nutmeg, grated (optional)

METHOD
Open brown cardamom pods, remove the seeds, and discard the peels. Break cinnamon stick into small pieces. On stove top, individually dry roast the black cumin seeds, brown cardamom seeds, black peppercorns, broken cinnamon pieces, and cloves in a heavy pan on medium heat. Roast the spices until they become fragrant, stirring them occasionally to evenly roast. Let them cool. Grind each spice separately in a coffee grinder. Mix all the

ground spices together and sift the mixture. Repeat the process until desired texture is achieved. Store garam masala in an airtight glass container in a cool and dry place. Garam masala can stay fresh for several months.

Ghee (Clarified butter)

Ghee is available in Indian food stores and in the ethnic section of some of grocery stores. (I discuss ghee extensively in Chapter 3, "Seasoning with Hot Ghee.") You can also make ghee at home following these instructions.

To prepare ghee, use a heavy-bottomed saucepan and unsalted butter. One pound of butter will make a little less then 2 cups of melted ghee.

To make ghee, melt butter over medium heat in a medium-size 2-quart, heavy-bottomed saucepan. Once the butter is melted, turn the heat to low and let the butter simmer slowly without letting it get brown. Continue to simmer on this slow heat until white froth forms on the surface. Gently stir the melted butter and reduce heat to the lowest point. Simmer uncovered until a creamy slush settles at the bottom of the pan and the slush changes to light brown. The melted, milky butter will change into the clear liquid called ghee; this process takes approximately 30 to 40 minutes. Remove the pan from the heat and cool.

Once the liquid is cool enough to handle, strain the ghee through a strainer lined with a paper towel. Discard the brown solids. Pour ghee into a glass jar with an airtight lid. Close the jar and store ghee in a cool place, like your basement. For longer storage, refrigerate or freeze.

Paneer

Paneer is freshly made cheese that you can prepare at home from regular milk. *Paneer* is used to make sweets and many curried dishes. It can also be purchased fresh or frozen at Indian and specialty food stores.

Here is my recipe for preparing paneer:

INGREDIENTS
8 cups or $1/2$ gallon 2% milk
$1/4$ cup lemon juice
2 teaspoons all-purpose flour

METHOD

Using a large, heavy saucepan, bring milk to a boil over high heat. When foam begins to rise, remove the pan from the heat and gently stir in the lemon juice. The milk will curdle and the milk solids will separate from the liquid whey (the watery part of the milk). Pour the entire contents into a large strainer set over a bowl lined with a cheesecloth. Run cold water over the cheese in the cloth. Once the *paneer* is cold enough to handle, squeeze the liquid out. Or you can wrap the cheesecloth around the *paneer* and tie it to the kitchen faucet. Let it hang there for a couple of hours so most of the liquid can drip into the sink, leaving the moist and soft *paneer*.

To make *paneer* cubes, remove *paneer* from the cloth and place in a bowl. Knead with 2 teaspoons of all-purpose flour until *paneer* forms a smooth ball. Place *paneer* on a flat surface over a damp cheesecloth. Spread to a $1/2$-inch thickness. Cover with another damp cheesecloth and top with a flat, heavy object for 3 to 4 hours to set the *paneer*. Cut into desired size and store in refrigerator up to 2 to 3 days, until ready to use, or freeze to keep for a longer time.

Peanuts

Some of my recipes call for using roasted ground peanuts. Roasted peanuts are sold in any grocery store or you can roast raw peanuts and grind them in a coffee grinder. Raw peanuts are available at many Asian and Indian food stores.

If you are using the store-bought roasted peanuts, buy the unsalted variety and grind them into a coarse powder using a coffee grinder. Place raw peanuts in a heavy-bottomed pan and roast them on medium-high heat, stirring often to avoid burning. Roast peanuts until they change to light brown and give the smell of roasted nuts.

If the raw peanuts have their skin, roast them the same way as above. Don't worry about the change in color. Continue roasting until you have an aroma of roasted nuts. Let the peanuts cool. Remove the skin by rubbing and pushing the skin off with both hands. Discard the skin. Grind the peanuts in a coffee grinder to desired coarseness. Store in the refrigerator to keep them fresh.

Rice

Rice is the most versatile grain used throughout India. Besides being an essential part of the daily diet, rice makes any meal complete when served with lentils, meat, and vegetables. The delicious snacks and desserts made with rice for special occasions attest to the importance of this grain to the culture of India. Some of the best rice in the country is produced in the northern region of India.

Of the many varieties of rice grown, each has its own qualities, degrees of softness, fragrance, and starch content. Because of its fragrance, the long grain basmati rice is the preferred rice for making *pullav*. When cooked, basmati rice becomes longer, more slender, and fluffy with a delightful aroma. This rice is available in Indian food stores or in either the ethnic or grain sections of grocery stores.

When buying basmati rice, look for the package that says "aged" rice. The older the basmati rice, the longer and fluffier it becomes when cooked. The cost varies according to its age, where it is produced, and quality. The best basmati rice comes from Dehra Dun, a city in the valley at the foothills of the Himalaya.

If you don't have basmati rice, you may substitute jasmine rice or any other long grain rice. Other long grain rice is a little sticky when cooked and does not increase in size as much as basmati rice. Long grain rice is often used in everyday cooking when softer rice is preferred.

With the following simple steps and a little common sense, you can cook perfect fluffy rice. Here are some of the most common observations and steps to follow to make tasty rice dishes.

PREPARING RICE FOR COOKING

1. Clean, wash, and soak rice 15 to 20 minutes before cooking. Wash rice with 3 to 4 changes of water until water runs clear. When washing rice, lightly rub the grains against each other with your hands. This step not only separates the grains, it also helps reduce starch content in the rice.

2. Select a wide pan, large enough to give the rice room to expand. Using a pan that's too small and deep results in packed, unevenly cooked, sticky rice. A 2-quart saucepan will have enough room for 1 cup of uncooked basmati rice. Normally 1 cup of aged, uncooked basmati rice produces about 3 to 4 cups of cooked rice, sufficient for 4 to 5 servings.

3. If cooking a large amount (more than 2 cups) of rice, cook the rice in smaller batches. If you choose to cook all the rice at the same time in one large pot, transfer portions of rice to serving platters as soon as it is cooked. Use large platters to let the steam escape from the rice and prevent overcooking. Cover platters loosely with foil or clean tea towels to keep the rice moist and warm.

4. To reheat rice, sprinkle it with a small amount of water. Loosely cover with plastic wrap or a lid. Microwave on high for 1 minute for each cup of cooked rice. If reheating on the stove, sprinkle rice with a small amount of water, use medium heat, and cover the pan with a lid. (The stove top method takes a longer time to fully reheat the rice.) Normally, rice is served steaming hot, but some rice dishes can be served at room temperature.

COOKING PERFECT RICE

1. Wash and soak 1 cup of basmati rice for 15 to 20 minutes.
2. Drain water from the rice using a strainer.
3. Place soaked rice with 1 1/2 cups to 2 cups of water (for desired softness) in a 2-quart pan on high heat. Bring rice to a boil. Reduce heat to medium-low; cover the pan, leaving a little gap to keep it from boiling over.
4. Cook for 8 to 9 minutes. By this time most of the water is absorbed and rice should feel soft when pressed between the fingers.
5. If you press the grain and it is brittle, cover the pan completely and reduce heat to lowest setting. Cook for another 3 to 4 minutes until desired softness is achieved.
6. Remove the pan from the stove and keep covered for 10 minutes. Gently fluff the rice with a fork before serving.
7. Use 1 tablespoon of lemon juice or butter when fluffing the rice to add great flavor and keep the rice separated.

Tamarind

Tamarind is a tropical fruit. The dry pod is about 3 to 5 inches long, tough in texture, and reddish brown in color. In India, only the mature and dried tamarind is used for cooking. You can find whole mature pods in grocery stores. In Indian stores and specialty stores, tamarind also comes as prepackaged blocks of compressed, seedless, and skinless tamarind, or as a concentrated paste.

Tamarind adds a sour taste to food. It is also used in making sweet and sour tamarind chutney.

Before using tamarind, break off the required amount from the block and soak it in hot water. When it is soft, use your hand to work with the fruit soaked in water to remove most of the pulp from the pods. Pass the pulp through a sieve to separate the fibers; save the pulp and discard the rest. The pulp will be used in cooking and making chutneys. It can be refrigerated 3 to 4 days or kept in the freezer up to 6 months. To make tamarind water, dilute 1 teaspoon of pulp with 2 tablespoons of water.

The tamarind concentrate is convenient to use, but take care to use only what the recipe calls for. Measure the required amount, add a few tablespoons of hot water, and let stand for a few minutes to soften the thick paste. Stir to make it smooth and ready for use.

SAMPLE MENUS

An Indian meal is as simple as a dish of lentils, seasoned vegetables, rice, and chapati. Or the meal can be an elaborate spread that includes several curries, an array of appetizers, an assortment of breads, different kinds of rice dishes, and, finally, wonderful, tempting sweets and desserts. And don't forget the complementary salads, *raitas*, chutneys, and pickles. An Indian menu varies greatly because of the diversity in religious practices and traditions in the different regions of India.

Traditionally, Indian food is not served in the successive courses you may be used to. For meals at home, food is served in individual bowls and arranged around a large round plate. The selection of food, including sweets, is served at the same time. For large gatherings, it is common to set all the food out on the table so guests can help themselves.

The recipes in this book cover much more then just the basic curries associated with Indian cooking. The menus in this chapter suggest suitable combinations. All you have to do is to mix and match to create the right combination for you.

Choose one recipe from the selection of crispy fritters. Match it with the chutney of your choice to serve as an appetizer or starter for a dinner party. Or serve these snacks as an accompaniment to afternoon tea. You can't go wrong even when you serve them in combination with a western menu.

For dinner, serve a meat curry or a vegetable curry over a selected rice dish for the main course. Combine this with one of the salads and a side dish of seasoned vegetables to complete the meal without much fuss.

For a simple lunch menu, choose one of the seasoned rice dishes and pair it with a cool *raita* and refreshing mango *lassi*. A brunch of puri and *chole* with sweet, fragrant Cream of Wheat *halwa* will keep you satisfied until dinnertime.

Plan your menu in advance. Prepare your curry, beans, and lentils a day in advance to give them time to absorb flavors and spices. You can reheat the curries and lentil dishes in the oven, on the stove, or in the microwave before serving.

If you plan to serve Indian bread, prepare the dough ahead of time. Make the bread a few hours before your guests arrive and then wrap it in aluminum foil to keep them warm. Reheat it in the microwave before serving.

Prepare salads, *raitas*, seasoned vegetables, and rice dishes fresh, unless a recipe instructs otherwise. Make your desserts and sweets in advance and have them ready to serve as advised in the recipe—hot, cold, or at room temperature.

Drinks should be prepared after your guests arrive. To retain freshness, make both cold and hot drinks just before serving.

Breakfast and Brunch Menus
Cream of Wheat Porridge
Spicy Corn Kernels
Mango Shake (summer) or Tea (winter)

Egg and Tomato Scramble
Spicy Deep-Fried Indian Bread
Potatoes with Cumin Seeds
Tea

Curried Garbanzo Beans
Deep-Fried Indian Bread
Cream of Wheat *Halwa*
Ginger Tea

Savory Pancakes
Coconut Chutney
Curried Dry Potatoes
Yogurt Drink

Lunch Menus
Pigeon Peas
Curried Zucchini in Peanut Sauce
  (over plain boiled rice)
Green Mustard and Radishes
Indian Flat Bread

Lemon Rice
Green Beans with Coconut
Roasted Eggplant with Yogurt
Coconut Slice

Red Kidney Beans
Rice with Cumin Seeds
Sprouted Mung Bean Salad
Fried Noodles Pudding

Lamb Curry with Cashews and Poppy Seeds
Saffron Rice
Cabbage and Tomato Salad
Eggplant Fritters
Yogurt Cheese and Saffron Pudding

Rice and Yellow Split Lentil Porridge
Cucumber with Yogurt
Dry Curried Potatoes I
Fish Curry
Litchi Yogurt Drink

Afternoon Tea and Snacks
Crispy Tortilla with Potatoes and Garbanzo Beans
Corn Fritters
Mint and Cilantro Chutney
Mango Shake

Potato-Stuffed Pastry
Tamarind Chutney
Mint and Cilantro Chutney
Tea

Potato Patty
Vegetable Fritters
Mint and Cilantro Chutney
Ginger Tea

Potato Puff Rolls
Mung Lentil Fritters
Fried Milk Balls in Syrup
Tea or Litchi Yogurt Drink

Dinner Menus
Curried Meat Balls
Stuffed Peppers
Brown Lentils
Carrot Salad
Indian Flat Bread
Fried Milk Balls in Syrup

Black-Eyed Peas
Eggplant and Mushroom Curry
Chicken in Peanut Sauce
Indian Flat Bread
Corn and Bell Pepper Rice
Rice Pudding

Cabbage *Kofta* Curry
Shrimp Curry
Yellow Split Lentils and Spinach
Tomatoes with Yogurt and Peanuts
Rice Pilaf with Mixed Vegetables
Coconut Slice

Egg Curry with Potatoes
Vegetable Delight
Butternut Squash with Yogurt
Lemon Rice
Oven-Baked *Roti* with Fenugreek Leaves
Fried Noodles Pudding

Curried Stuffed Tomatoes
Carrots and Peas Curry
Red Lentils
Roasted Eggplant with Yogurt
Deep-Fried Indian Bread
Yogurt Cheese and Saffron Pudding

Potatoes and Peas Curry
Stuffed Okra with Onions
Seasoned Mung Beans
Spicy Deep-Fried Indian Bread
Yogurt Rice
Cream of Wheat *Halwa*

Glossary

Aalu (aloo, alu) Potato.

Aam Mango.

Adrak Ginger.

Ajwayan (ajawain) Brownish green, small, ridged seeds with pungent taste. Used in many savory dishes and used as a cure for stomach ailments.

Arhar dal (toor dal) Type of lentil used extensively in India, also known as pigeon peas. The lentil is yellow in color, available plain or coated with oil to extend its shelf life.

Ande Eggs.

Ankur Sprouts.

Asafetida (asafoitida) Strong-smelling dried gum resins from the roots of a plant in the fennel family. Also known as *hing* in Hindi. Often used in Indian cooking to enhance taste and as a substitute for onions and garlic.

Ayurvedic An ancient Hindu science of health and medicine. A Sanskrit word.

Baingan Eggplant.

Burfi A variety of sweet made of milk, sugar, lentil flour, and nuts. Also spelled *barfi*.

Basmati rice Fragrant variety of long grain rice. Some of the best is from the foothills of the Himalayas.

Besan Variety of flour made from chickpeas, garbanzo beans, or from a variety of chickpea known as *kala-chana*. The flour is used for making snacks and sweets.

Bhari Stuffed.

Bhatura, pl. bhature Deep-fried bread made with fermented all-purpose flour.

Bharvan subji Stuffed vegetables.

Bhurta Dish made from roasted, mashed, and seasoned eggplant or potatoes.

Bhindi Okra.

Bhune Roasted.

Bhurji Food that is scrambled, as in scrambled eggs.

Chaat Variety of spicy snacks served by street vendors.

Chaat masala Spicy hot and sour mixture of spices used over fruit salads, vegetables, potatoes, and chickpeas.

Chai Hot drink prepared with water, milk, sugar, and tea leaves and flavored with ginger, cardamom, or other herbs or spices.

Chakki A grinding stone consisting of two circular slabs of stone with a handle. Used for grinding grain into flour and making spice powders.

Chana **dal** Yellow split peas.

Chapati, pl. chapatis Flat Indian bread made with unleavened wheat flour, cooked on an iron griddle, and served hot with ghee. Also known as *roti*.

Chawal (chaaval) Cooked or uncooked rice.

Chilke wali dal Split lentils with skin.

Chole Cooked or uncooked chickpeas or garbanzo beans. A very popular dish made with garbanzo beans is also known as *chole*.

Chote Small.

Chounk Indian word used to describe a method of seasoning using hot oil or ghee, combined with a variety of spices to give special flavor and aroma to a dish. *Tadka, fodni,* and *vaghar* are some other words used to describe this technique.

Chounki Seasoned.

Chutney, pl. chutneys Spicy condiment prepared with herbs, spices, nuts, and fruits.

Chutni See chutney.

Cilantro Fresh coriander.

Coriander seeds The seeds are yellowish brown in color, spherical in shape, and slightly smaller than whole black peppercorns. The seeds impart a roasted, earthy smell when cooked in hot oil or dry roasted.

Curry The English pronunciation for the Indian word *kari*. The word refers to a method of cooking vegetables and meat using special blends of spices. Indians also use the word "curry" for sauce or gravy.

Curry leaves Aromatic leaves of the plant also known as *kari patta*. Used in seasoning to add flavor to a variety of dishes.

Curry paste See *masala*.

Dal *(dahl)* Beans and lentils.

Dahi Yogurt.

Dahi-wada *Urad* lentil dumpling soaked in yogurt sauce and topped with tamarind chutney. A savory snack dish. See also *urad dal.*

Desiccated coconut Unsweetened, finely shredded, dehydrated coconut.

Dhania Coriander. *See also* coriander seeds.

Dhuli **dal** Split lentils without skin. See also *dhuli moong.*

Dhuli moong Split mung beans without skin. See also *dhuli dal.*

Dosa Thin, crispy pancakes prepared with ground, fermented rice, and *urad* lentil batter.

Faliyan Green beans.

Fenugreek Annual herb also known as *methi* in Hindi. The yellow seeds become fragrant when roasted in oil and have a bitter taste. The herb is also used fresh and dried in Indian cooking.

Fodni See *chounk.*

Gajar Carrots.

Garam masala Spice mixture made with cinnamon, cardamom, black pepper, and cloves. Frequently used in the cooking of northern India.

Ghee Clarified butter. Ghee is made by heating unsalted butter until milk solids separate from the butter fat and settle at the bottom of the pan. Butter fat (ghee) is strained and milk solids are discarded.

Gobhi Cauliflower.

Gulab-jamun Fried milk balls soaked in sugar syrup. A popular sweet.

Haldi Turmeric.

Halwa (halva) Generic name for a sweet made from a variety of flours, grains, lentils, vegetables, and fruits.

Hamam Dasta Mortar and pestle used for grinding herbs and spices.

Hari Green.

Hara dhania See cilantro.

Hindi Official language of India. Mainly spoken in northern India.

Hing See asafetida.

Imli See tamarind.

Jeera, **pl.** *Jeere* Cumin seeds.

Jhinga Shrimp.

Kaddu Butternut squash.

Kadhi A dish made with yogurt and chickpea flour.

Kaju Cashew nut.

Kala-chana A variety of chickpea, smaller than a chickpea in size and black in color.

Kari patta See curry leaves.

Kesar Saffron.

Kheer Milk pudding, prepared by simmering milk with different types of grains, seeds, vegetables, fruits, and nuts.

Kheera, **pl.** *kheere* Cucumber.

Khumbhi Mushrooms.

Khus-khus Poppy seeds.

Khichri Mixture of rice and lentils cooked together with spices.

Kirana Supply store that sells grains, spices, oil, sugar, and other dry food items.

Kofta, **pl.** *kofte* Deep-fried ground meat and vegetable balls.

Korma Thick sauce prepared with nuts and spices.

Kulcha Oven baked. See *tandoor.* Unleavened bread made with all-purpose flour. *Kulcha* can be plain or stuffed with various fillings.

Lal Red.

Lal **dal** Red lentils.

Lassi Cool, frothy yogurt drink served with ice. *Lassi* can be sweet or salty and is served in many fruit flavors such as mango and litchi.

Leechi See litchi.

Lentils Flat, edible seeds of a plant from the family *Leguminosae.*

Lobia (lobhia) Black-eyed peas. Also known as *rongi* and *chowli.*

Litchi A tropical, oval fruit of the soapberry family. The fruit has hard scaly skin, a hard seed, and edible sweet, firm flesh. Also known as lychee.

Machli Fish.

Makka Corn.

Makki Corn grain.

Masala Hindi word for spices. *Masala* may refer to just one spice or a combination of spices. It may also refer to ground fresh ingredients used in preparing various sauces for curries. For example, garam masala is a blend of several spices. Onion *masala* is a ground mixture of onion, ginger, and garlic used in preparing various meat and vegetable curries. It is a generic term for spices, spice mixtures, or fresh ingredients cooked with spices.

Masoor (masar) Brown lentils.

Matar Peas.

Methi *See* fenugreek.

Mili Mixed.

Mirch Fresh, dried, and powdered chili pepper.

Moong (mung, mug) A variety of whole lentils with cylindrical beans and green skin.

Moong **dal** Split mung beans with skin.

Moongfali Peanuts.

Mukh-vas Mouth freshener. Offered as a conclusion to a meal.

Muli Radish.

Murgi Chicken.

Naan Oven-baked leavened flat bread. Naan can be plain, stuffed, or flavored with fresh herbs and aromatic seeds. *See tandoor.*

Nariyal Coconut.

Neembu Lemon.

Oothuppum Savory pancakes.

Paan Betel leaf and betel leaf packets with a variety of fillings. Chewed after a meal as a stimulant and digestive aid.

Paan-dan A specially designed container for *paan* and other necessary ingredients.

Pakora, **pl.** *pakoras* Deep-fried vegetable fritters made with chickpea flour and assorted vegetables.

Palak Spinach.

Paneer Homemade cheese prepared by curdling milk with lemon. Milk solids separate from the whey and the liquid is drained. The milk solids (*paneer*) are used in making a variety of sweets and curries.

Pappadum Thin, crispy, round lentil wafers. Made from a variety of lentils and spices. Also known as *papad* in northern India.

Paratha Pan-fried, unleavened flat bread made with whole wheat flour and fried with oil or ghee. *Paratha* can be plain or stuffed. They vary in shape from round, triangular, and rectangular plain *paratha* to round stuffed *paratha*.

Patta Leaf.

Patta-gobhi Cabbage.

Pilaf (pulau) See *pullav*.

Piyaz Onion.

Peesa Ground.

Pudina, **pl.** *pudine* Mint.

Pullav Seasoned rice dish with vegetables or meat. Also known as pilaf or *pulau*.

Puri (poori), **pl.** **puris** Deep-fried, puffed, round bread prepared with unleavened whole wheat flour and fried in hot oil using a wok.

Raai (rai) Black mustard seeds.

Raita, **pl.** *raitas* Yogurt dish prepared by mixing raw or cooked vegetables and fruits in yogurt that is mildly seasoned with spices.

Rajma Red kidney beans.

Rasa, **pl.** *rase* Gravy or sauce in a curry.

Rase ki subji Vegetable dish with a light gravy.

Rongi See *lobia*.

Roti See *chapati*.

Rus Juice.

Sabat moong Whole mung beans.

Saffron Bright orange, aromatic flower stigmas used to flavor and color food.

Sambhar A seasoned lentil dish from southern India, prepared with a variety of vegetables, coconut, and tamarind.

Sambhar masala Spice mix used for preparing *sambhar*. See also *sambhar*.

Samosa Triangular shaped, deep-fried pastry stuffed with seasoned potatoes and peas or with seasoned and cooked meat.

Sanskrit An ancient language from India. Most Hindu scriptures are written in Sanskrit. See also *Vedas* and *Vedic*.

Sarson Mustard.

Seviyan (sevian) Fine noodles, used with milk to make pudding.

Shimla A place up north in India. Also refers to bell pepper (*shimla mirch*).

Shorba The word *shorba* is an Urdu word meaning soup, broth, gravy, or sauce.

Shrikhand Yogurt pudding, made with yogurt cheese, sugar, fruits, and nuts.

Sooji Cream of Wheat or semolina.

Sookha, **pl.** *sookhe* Dry.

Sookhi subji Vegetables cooked in spices and oil with no gravy.

Subji Hindi word for vegetables. The word *subji* is used for both cooked and uncooked vegetables.

Supari Areca nut also known as betel nut. One of the essential ingredients for *paan* and *mukhvas*.

Tadka See *chounk*.

Tamatar Tomato.

Tamarind A tropical fruit used as a souring agent for many dishes and chutneys.

Tandoor Clay oven used in baking a variety of Indian breads and cooking meat dishes referred to as tandoori dishes.

Tandoori Food cooked in a tandoor is referred to as tandoori. See also *tandoor*.

Tel Oil.

Tikki Patty.

Toor dal See *arhar dal*.

Tortilla Mexican bread made with all-purpose flour or cornmeal. In the United States, tortillas are available in grocery stores or at Mexican specialty food stores.

Ubtan Mixture of flour, oil, and turmeric. Used as cleanser for the body and face.

Umbelliferae Group name for plants in the parsley and carrot family.

Upma Spicy Cream of Wheat porridge.

Urad dal (*urd*) A variety of split lentils with black skin also known as black gram.

Vaghar See *chounk*.

Vedas Hindu scriptures. Written in ancient language Sanskrit.

Vedic Hindu history and culture between 1500 B.C. and 500 B.C.

Whey Watery part of the milk separated from milk solids during the process of making cheese.

Yellow split lentil See *dhuli moong*.

Bibliography

Devi, Yamuna. *Lord Krishna's Cuisine: The Art of Indian Vegetarian Cooking*. New York: E.P. Dutton, 1987.

Gadia, Madhu. *Lite and Luscious Cuisine of India*. Ames: Piquant Publishing, 1997.

Jaffrey, Madhur. *Madhur Jaffrey's World Vegetarian*. New York: Clarkson Potter/Publishers, 1999.

Peterson, Joan, and Indu Menon. *Eat Smart in India*. Madison: Ginkgo Press Inc., 2004.

Rau, Santha Rama. *The Cooking of India*. New York: Time-Life Books Inc., 1969.

Singh, Balbir (Mrs). *Mrs. Balbir Singh's Indian Cookery*. London: Mills and Boon Limited, 1975.

Recipe Index

Vegetables